OLIVIA

One Woman's Journey

Darren Mason

MINERVA PRESS
ATLANTA   LONDON   SYDNEY

OLIVIA: *One Woman's Journey*
Copyright © Darren Mason 1999

All Rights Reserved

ISBN 0 75410 817 1

First Published 1999 by
MINERVA PRESS
315–317 Regent Street
London W1R 7YB

Printed in Great Britain for Minerva Press

OLIVIA
One Woman's Journey

This book is dedicated to Vicki – a fellow spirit – whose love, friendship and guidance transcends three continents.
From my heart to yours, with love.
Also to the woman who has been my inspiration for over two decades – Olivia Newton-John – the voice behind the face.
And, by no means last, for Aggy – my dearly missed Nan – who always believed in my dreams.

Acknowledgements

The writing of this book would not have been possible without the help of many television and radio interviews, and the kind and generous time devoted by the former teachers with Victoria's Education Department in Australia. Also *Only Olivia*, the international fan club for their help and support. Data for *Facts and Figures* section courtesy of *The Guinness Book of British Hit Singles and Albums*, *Billboard Magazine* USA and *Australian Chart Research*. The *Universal Pictorial Press and Agency Ltd* (London); *Picture Archives* at Melbourne's *Sun-Herald* newspaper; ipc Magazines Limited (London); Andre Deutsch Ltd (London); and ACP Publishing Pty Limited (Australia).

Photo on front cover courtesy of MCA/Geffen Records.

About the Author

Darren Mason was born in Hinckley, Leicestershire in December 1966. Having become an ardent Olivia Newton-John fan in the mid-Seventies, he has devoted his time to following every step of her career taking the initiative in 1992 to launch *Only Olivia*, an unofficial fan magazine dedicated to introducing her fans to the real Olivia Newton-John. His decision to write as complete a biography as possible was borne out of a desire to give her the accolade she so deserves.

Introduction

I was diagnosed with breast cancer on July 3rd, 1992. Not only am I a survivor, but I have never felt stronger physically or spiritually... this is my journey.

Olivia Newton-John, 1994

When the headlines in July of 1992 revealed the news that Olivia Newton-John had cancer, the whole world stopped in disbelief. Any pop icon, movie star or person in the public eye is always the last person you expect to 'suffer' from any major illness. Yet, here we were, all reading of the fresh-faced, girl-next-door star of *Grease*, fighting her biggest battle to date.

Until that point, Olivia's only battles, and triumphs, had been in her career – she had proved the cynics wrong when they wrote that her music was bland and lacking emotion, by going to America and becoming a national institution both on record and on the cabaret circuit. She earned no less than twenty-four gold discs and eight platinum over the ensuing two decades. No easy feat for the girl they labelled 'the singing milkshake' whose only talents were her looks!

'Ambition' had always appeared to be a 'dirty' word, especially where women were concerned, but Olivia knew what she wanted to do. Although, at an earlier age she had considered a career in veterinary surgery – 'I was never very good at maths or science, so that knocked that on the head!' she says; and had also thought about joining Melbourne's Mounted Police Force, that way she could have a job and be paid for enjoying her favourite pastime – horse riding. Victorian State laws in the Sixties did not permit women into that area of their forces, so that put paid to that ambition.

Olivia went on to become one of the most instantly recognisable faces of the entertainment industry. The majority of people recognising her as 'the girl who was in *Grease*' or 'didn't she sing that song "Physical"?' Our more mature audiences exclaim: 'I remember her when she used to sing with Cliff Richard in the Seventies!' But, what a lot of people don't realise is, 'Lovely Livvy' was a regional success in Australia before she had even left high school!

Her face, double-barrelled name and voice were regularly seen on television screens in her adopted home town of Melbourne, making her professional singing debut on Channel Nine's *Sunnyside Up* variety show, in 1963, with a cover version of a Liza Minnelli song and earning her first fifty-pound pay packet. With guest appearances on *The Go Show* and *Time for Terry*, it wasn't long before young Olivia was well established in the hearts of Australian audiences.

Had it not been for her first prize trip to England, following a talent quest in 1965, what would have become of Olivia Newton-John is unknown. Would success on local television have catapulted her to international stardom? Would a recording contract have come her way and put her at the top of Australia's music charts?

Luckily, she took that trip to London and tentatively made her recording debut with Decca Records in 1966. Unfortunately, not a resounding success – it never made it past the demo stage – but it laid the foundations for what was to come as the next decade got into its stride.

A meteoric rise to superstardom is nothing more than an understatement. Finding instant success in Britain following a regular guest spot on the BBC's *It's Cliff Richard*, and then taking America by storm on the wave of a top ten hit, 'Let Me Be There', in 1973, Hollywood has certainly brought Olivia Newton-John OBE all that she had ever dreamt of. 'I used to read about all these big stars and think life must be perfect once you've got a big bank account, a great house and servants.'

'Life must be wonderful,' she said to Britain's *TV Times* in 1980. 'And then when you get there you realise you're no different, you're the same person. You have luxuries but you don't have people because they see the illusion created around your name before they see you.'

In 1975, Olivia was to take complete control over her career when she became a 'self-made' business and Olivia Newton-John Enterprises came into being, making Olivia one of the first singer/performers to be under contract with a record label and yet own the copyright to all of the tracks she recorded and their respective albums. This may explain why, after thirty years in show business, no authorised collection of rare or unreleased material has ever appeared as with fellow performers Barbra Streisand, Diana Ross, Neil Diamond and Cliff Richard. Olivia showed early signs of the shrewd businesswoman that would eventually come into her own ten years later with Koala Blue.

In the ensuing decade, Olivia would go on to sell in excess of fifty million records worldwide, besides the ever-popular, multi-platinum selling *Grease* soundtrack album in 1978. She achieved success not only on the big screen, but also on television with two ratings winning TV movies and a wildlife show for Australia's Channel Nine network in the Nineties.

Now, as a new millennium approaches, and Olivia

Newton-John enters her fourth decade in show business, is there anything more for this multi-talented person to try her hand at? As the blockbuster movie *Grease* receives its twentieth anniversary re-release, going into the American top five in its first week, and the launch of a new album of country songs, 1999 looks as though she has put her battles of the last five years well and truly behind her and is ready to take on the world again.

PART ONE

If you set out to create the typical 'Aussie girl' who was fresh, pretty, bright and open, full of life and fun, you would definitely finish up with Olivia Newton-John! I guess that's why she became Australia's favourite girl.

Ray Martin, Australian TV journalist

Wherever I Lay My Hat...

Home for Olivia Newton-John has always been wherever her heart is, whether on her palatial, self-designed beach-front home in Malibu or her eighty-acre avocado farm in Byron Bay, Australia. But it was on a mild Sunday morning, September 26th, 1948, in the old university town of Cambridge, England, that Olivia was born.

Olivia was the last of three children (following Hugh and Rona) born to Bryn Newton-John and his German-born wife Irene. They lived comfortably in a small terraced cottage in St Peter's Terrace, Cambridge, where Welsh-born Bryn was a lecturer at King's College.

Academia certainly ran in the family – with Irene being the daughter of a renowned German physicist, Max Born, who claimed Albert Einstein as a close friend and was one of the famous three to split the atom. He was born December 11th, 1882, in Bresslau, Germany to academic parents and studied at both Heidelberg and Zurich Universities before becoming a lecturer himself in 1915, in Berlin. 1933 brought him to Cambridge, where he was to lecture for the next four years in Applied Mathematics. He published an autobiography in 1968, but his work was officially recognised with the Nobel Prize for Physics in 1954.

'I know this sounds terrible,' recalls Olivia, 'but I have so little knowledge of what he actually did, because it was so complicated. But he was a very brilliant man. I wish I had known him. Although I did meet him once, briefly, when I was very young.'

He was to pass away through natural causes on January 5th, 1970, in Pyrmont, Germany – a year before Olivia was to hit the big time!

Olivia was a quiet child and very protective of those close to her. She possessed an abundant love of animals: 'As a young girl, I didn't really have a best friend. I was always friends with the dog next door. I was always bringing home strays and telling people off for mistreating animals.'

In October of 1953, not long after Olivia's fifth birthday, the Newton-John family left England, bound for Australia, where Bryn had accepted the post of Dean of Ormond College in Melbourne. The sailing took just under three months, finally docking in Port Melbourne on January 26th, 1954. A date that remains special to the family for two reasons: it was Australia Day and it was also Rona's birthday.

Adapting to her new life 'down under' was hard. Due to Bryn Newton-John's new position, the family had to live on campus, which prevented Olivia fulfilling her need to care for nature's waifs and strays. Also, the constant taunting from school friends about her 'Pommie' accent made her feel like an outsider.

Remembering Days of the Old School Yard...

Olivia's formative years were spent at The Rural School, a teacher training section of Melbourne's Teachers College. Miss M.F. Williams recalls: 'I taught Olivia through grades four, five and six. The students were drawn from the local areas of Parkville, Carlton and a few from University Colleges, as with Olivia.' All students who attended The Rural School went swimming most Wednesdays during the year at the Old Melbourne Baths on Swanston Street and participated in interschool swimming galas.

'Like all students, Olivia was involved with singing, recorder and would have taken her turn at being monitor for the lower grades,' continues Miss Williams. 'She would have developed self-organisation and responsibility. It would be unfair to say that she stood out from any of the others in Music, English or Sport; but clearly she was able, co-operative and pleasant. I saw her then as developing into a well-adjusted young lady.'

'We had to arrive at school by nine o'clock and then you went to chapel for half an hour before lessons, for prayers and hymns. I got used to that – it was everyday life,' recalled Olivia during an interview with America's Tom Cohn in 1980. 'I remember one day, during a religious instruction lesson, I asked the Reverend a question, and he couldn't really give me a constructive answer, and it didn't make sense to me. From that day on I lost interest in it and didn't believe any more. I was due to be confirmed about a month later, but I told my mother I couldn't go through with it.'

Dawn Carty, who in 1958 was junior secretary in the Bacteriology Department at the university, recalls: 'Olivia's father and Professor Sydney Rubbo (whom Olivia affectionately referred to as "Uncle Syd") were the best of friends, and she would often stop off at the office on her way home from school where she would cause chaos.' She continued, 'We had animals attached to our department so she would be out playing with those or dancing and singing around the corridors or playing in her father's study where she would draw on his blackboard, sometimes creating space by rubbing off his scientific calculations and formulae.'

During the summer of 1958/59 (the summer season in the southern hemisphere runs from October through March), one of Melbourne's leading cinema chains held a contest for the girl who most looked like Hayley Mills (star of Walt Disney's film *Pollyanna*). Unbeknown to ten-year-old Livvy, Rona sent in her sister's picture, and she won! The prize was a set of theatre passes.

'They were very crafty,' says Olivia, 'you couldn't go on weekends or during holidays. So when was a ten-year-old able to go to the movies?'

Despite young Livvy's first taste of 'fame', 1959 was not the best of times. Having been in the country for only five years, Bryn and Irene decided to separate and later divorced, a situation that was unheard of at that time in Australia. Bryn had no choice but to resign from his post at the college, as they didn't allow divorced faculty members to remain on staff, and Irene moved into an apartment on the other side of town, taking Olivia with her. By this time, both Hugh and Rona had married.

'It was difficult,' recalls Olivia. 'As a child, you think it was somehow your fault. I wanted to be with my Mum and Dad, but they lived apart and I had to go with Mum. My father was a classical music fan, and for years after their divorce, whenever I heard classical music, I always associated it with sadness.'

Her sister, Rona, comments: 'It was very hard for Olivia, being the only child left at home. Both myself and Hugh had married. She called herself "the latch-key kid", because Mum would still be at work when she got in from school.'

It was whilst attending Christchurch Grammar School (and later University High), along with a young student by the name of Daryl Braithwaite, who would later find international fame himself, as lead singer with Australian-based band *Sherbert*, that the initial seeds for performing were sown, when Olivia gave a fine performance in George Bernard Shaw's play *Poison, Passion and Putrefaction* in 1961. She played the maid, a part which, coincidentally, attracted praise from the harsh drama critics of the High School's magazine *UBIQUE*. She then went on to appear in another school production, this time of J.M. Barrie's *The Admirable Crichton*, which promised to be her best performance so far. A review appeared in the magazine saying: 'Olivia as Lady Mary, acted perfectly, giving just the right idea of the English drawing-room.' In the July 15th, 1964 edition of the magazine, they printed an interview with Olivia.

> *Reporter*: Olivia, when did you really start taking an interest in the theatre?
> *Olivia*: July 16th, 1950 at six o'clock in the morning.
> *Reporter*: Is it true you are English?
> *Olivia*: Yes, I was born in Cambridge.
> *Reporter*: What are your favourite types of music?

Olivia:	All kinds – from classical to pop.
Reporter:	What's your opinion of The Beatles?
Olivia:	Sweet, but nothing to go to pieces over. I'll send you their regards from England when I get there.

In the meantime, Olivia teamed up with three girlfriends to become The Sol Four, singing traditional jazz at local clubs, until her mother decided their school work was beginning to suffer and they disbanded. However, Olivia was still allowed to visit her brother-in-law's coffee bar on weekends, where he had a resident folk singer.

'It kind of happened by accident really. I used to join in, singing harmonies. Until one night Hans invited me up on stage and I ended up doing a solo slot,' remembers Olivia.

She continued to perform with Hans at the coffee bar, and after one particular performance, a member of the audience, veteran Australian entertainer Horrie Dargie, suggested she enter a local television talent quest. With Rona's encouragement, Olivia entered, won her heat and went on to win the final of *Sing! Sing! Sing!*, hosted by Australia's wild man – Johnny O'Keefe, with her inimitable version of *Everything's Coming Up Roses*.

No one was less surprised at her winning than local TV presenter, Bert Newton: 'It was a Sunday night, my wife and I were watching *Sing! Sing! Sing!* with Johnny O'Keefe, and there was this young girl, and I said, "She'll win it!" – and she did! Although probably more for her looks than her voice.'

At that time, Olivia was still at school, and along with the prize of a trip to England came offers of television work, but her mother wanted her to finish school first. Even the local press became involved, printing pictures of her in school uniform and on TV with captions: 'School or Stardom?' It became, in a sense, a public trial.

It was on the advice of Olivia's favourite teacher, who said: 'If you are going to be thinking about singing, you are never going to make it through your final year. So, follow what you want to do,' that she made her choice. By Olivia's own admission she wasn't 'one of the brightest of pupils. I didn't concentrate very well at school. I think I was capable – I had the brain power, I just didn't have the concentration. I was always terribly confused by everything. Sometimes I wish I could start school now because I'd probably benefit from it a whole lot more now.'

Irene was not pleased by this decision. She approached Brian Goldsmith, Rona's husband, to talk to young Livvy and hopefully convince her to continue with her Higher School Certificate. Brian eventually suggested taking Livvy to one of the best teachers in Melbourne to assess her singing ability. After only one session Olivia was set against the idea, complaining, 'he wants to change the way I sing!'

Almost eighteen months were to pass before Olivia took advantage of her prize trip to London. In the meantime, she accepted invitations to appear on local television, with guest spots on *Bandstand*, *Time for Terry* and *The Go Show*, where she met and became friends with fellow up-and-coming hopefuls Pat Carroll and John Farrar.

Television presenter and friend, Ian Turpie says: 'In 1964, television was an integral part of the Australian music industry, and many personalities gained recognition and prominence from appearing on such as *The Go Show*.'

Funny Things Happen...

In the spring of 1965, Olivia was signed up by Pacific Films, a New Zealand-based company, to appear in a film to be directed by Joe McCormick featuring The Terrible Ten. The comedy, *Funny Things Happen Down Under*, was a sequel to The Terrible Ten's successful television series which began in 1964.

The Ten, a group of country children from Wallaby Creek, are trying to save their headquarters, an old woolshed, from demolition. They accidentally discover a formula that causes sheep to grow coloured wool, but then have great difficulty in convincing adults that their multicoloured sheep are genuine. The story ends on a happy note, though, when, at a Christmas party, the winners of a shearing contest donate their prize-money to save the woolshed.

The movie was filmed on location in the Melbourne area and in Pacific's studios. Howard Morrison, a Maori singer, was flown in to appear as a shearer and to sing several songs. Ian Turpie also sang and acted in the film along with Olivia, who sang one song, 'Christmas Down Under'.

It was premiered in August 1965 in provincial cinemas across New Zealand, before being presented at the Commonwealth Arts Festival, London, in September. Unable to attract a commercial distributor for Australia, Pacific released the film themselves at the Princes Theatre in Melbourne, in December 1966.

By that time, however, Olivia had begrudgingly taken up her prize trip to England, accompanied by her mother. Olivia just didn't want to be in London! She had fallen in love with Ian Turpie whilst filming the previous year, and wanted to be with him.

A clash of personalities between Turpie and Mrs Newton-John – she felt threatened by this handsome young man who was about to whisk off her young Livvy, and he was the strong-willed young performer determined to make a success of himself – meant that Irene was insistent that the experience of London would broaden her daughter's horizons. Olivia still wasn't convinced, sneaking out of their rented flat in London's Shepherd's Bush, down to a local travel agent and booking a return flight to Melbourne, only to be followed by her mother moments later to cancel it.

'I tried that escape on more than one occasion,' says Olivia, 'and each time Mum would go in later in the day saying – has she been in again?' At one point she visited a lawyer in the hope of being made a ward of court, but was promptly informed that her mother still had legal control over her.

She eventually gave in and, in April 1966, auditioned for and signed a one-off single deal with Decca Records. The previous year, an American singer/songwriter from Kentucky, by the name of Jackie de Shannon, had flown in to London to search for possible vocalists as vehicles for her songs. She had recently had success with the Searchers' version of 'When You Walk in the Room', and assigned 'Daydreaming of You' to the Hellions and was now promoting a new song – 'Till You Say You'll Be Mine', which went to Olivia.

The track, with no named producer and heavy Motown-orientated arrangement was an ambitious start for

Livvy's maiden single. With its stomping rhythm section and decidedly under-produced vocals, 'Till You Say You'll Be Mine' was only issued as a demonstration disc, featuring the song 'Forever',[1] with its dainty dual-tracked harmonies, as the flip-side. Even the appearance of a publicity photograph by David Wedgbury failed to help get the single on to radio play lists.

It was certainly a challenge for eighteen-year-old Olivia. Breaking on to the British music scene in the Sixties – particularly by a solo female vocalist – was a huge task, especially with fellow teenagers Sandie Shaw, Helen Shapiro and Lulu (who had scored with Decca Records two years earlier on a cover version of the Isley Brothers' 'Shout') having already stamped their presence on the UK charts, and each one offering a unique vocal style.

---

[1] Both tracks eventually found their way on to a compilation CD of lost 45s of the Sixties entitled: *Pop Inside The Sixties* on the See For Miles label in 1993, alongside other hopefuls David Essex, The Orchids, Pinkertons Colours and Tony Wilson, to name a few.

One and One – Makes Success...

Not long after her first venture into the recording studio (although she had been featured on a demonstration disc for BEA – Broadcast Exchange of Australia – in 1965 on a cover version of The Animals' 'House of the Rising Sun' which had never made it on to record), Olivia met up with fellow Aussie and friend Pat Carroll. Two years older than Olivia, Pat had been moderately successful in the Australian charts with the single 'He's My Guy', and in the musical comedy stage shows 'Bye Bye Birdie' and 'Carnival', had recently won a radio award trip to London. With Irene's encouragement, the girls decided to team up and become a double act. After Irene returned home, Olivia and Pat moved into a flat in the Earls Court area of London, feeling well at home. That particular area is popular with Australians and was known as 'Little Australia'.

Having formed the duo 'Pat and Olivia', they set about finding work. They toured army bases around the country as well as nightclub venues in London. Pat has a memory of one particular gig at Raymond's Revue Bar in Soho: 'We were waiting in this smoke-filled room to go on, and on stage was this girl in a fish tank taking her clothes off! Then we went out in our cute little lace dresses up to the neck and cut just above the knee, and started singing 'September in the Rain'. We sang the one song and the manager paid us and said not to bother coming back.'

Thankfully, London's seedy nightlife didn't deter the two girls. By the end of 1966, they were the support act on the national tour of fellow Australians The Seekers and had also been signed up by the BBC to appear on its very popular *Dick Emery Show*. However, Mr Emery wasn't too impressed with their names, so for the duration of their contract they were billed as 'Liza and Jane'.

It appears that Dick Emery wasn't the only one who had a problem with their names. Britain's Des O'Connor remembers his first encounter with the duo: 'I've always had an eye out for new acts, and I first heard Pat and Olivia at an audition at the Prince of Wales Theatre in the West End. They sang well with good harmonies, and after they'd finished we went for a coffee. Olivia mentioned that they didn't have anything to rehearse with, so I took them up to Tottenham Court Road and bought them a cassette player.'

'I remember thinking that the name "Pat Carroll and Olivia Newton-John" was a bit long for a double act – they'd be running late before they had finished announcing them!' He continues, 'I actually suggested they rename themselves "The Poppettes". They were the catchy type of names acts used in the Sixties!'

By 1967, 'Pat and Olivia' were firmly establishing themselves on the British cabaret scene. That summer they were asked to join The Shadows in their summer shows in Bournemouth, where they met up with Britain's favourite male singer – Cliff Richard. A strong bond formed not only between Olivia and Cliff, but also between Olivia and Bruce Welch (bass guitarist with The Shadows). A romance blossomed and in a much publicised affair, twenty-year-old Olivia was named as 'the other woman' in the divorce proceedings with Welch's wife.

The young couple moved into a flat in south-west London, overlooking Lord's cricket ground. It certainly looked as though Olivia had found true love. 'Bruce was separated at the time, although that doesn't make it right, but we were happy together,' recalls Olivia.

Being with Bruce meant that Olivia, a naive twenty years of age, along with Pat Carroll, Cliff and the rest of The Shadows, found herself mixing with the music world's top names. One of whom was Paul McCartney. 'One day we went round to Paul's house and he said, "I've just written this song," and then started playing "Lady Madonna",' says Olivia. 'At the time, I didn't even realise what I was hearing, I was so thrilled to be meeting Paul. When I look back, it's amazing to think that I was actually there when he wrote that song!'

Following their successful season supporting The Shadows, Pat and Olivia seemed as though they could do no wrong. They teamed up with Cliff Richard as support act/backing vocalists on his 1968 tour of the Far East.

Cliff recalls, 'I remember at one point, I was performing one of my songs, and yet the audience were focused on Livvy and Pat behind me. They had been working on this routine and before I knew what was happening, they were in front of me! I had to fight my way back through them!'

A live recorded album of the concerts was eventually issued by Cliff's record label, EMI, in 1972 titled: *Cliff Goes East with Olivia Newton-John*, although Olivia, along with Pat Carroll, could only be heard on backing vocals. Then, when the tour ended, the duo returned to Britain, only to be informed that Pat's visa had expired and she had no option but to go back to Melbourne. Leaving Olivia, once again, to pursue a solo career.

And Then *Toomorrow* Came...

Bruce Welch began to take an active part in Olivia's career at this point: Peter Gormley, Cliff's manager, was interested in working with Olivia. So Welch set out looking for material.

Back in 1965, record producer Don Kirschner had successfully created The Monkees, along with their hit television show. He now thought the timing was right to try and repeat what had already been a successful formula and 'manufacture' another group along similar lines for a future project. The idea was to create the world's first all-purpose, multi-racial group offering something for everyone. At the time it was said that the group was formed from 'the fruits of six months' research' and that the 'findings were sifted by computer analysis'.

Three of the four members had already been signed: Benny Thomas from America and Vic Cooper and Chris Slade from London; although Slade would only feature on the group's debut single release ('I Could Never Live Without Your Love' on DECCA Records, issued August 1970) and would later be replaced by Afro-American Karl Chambers for the film. Kirschner was now looking for a girl to complete the line-up and was originally considering Ben's girlfriend, Susan George, but then he heard of Olivia. Before any final decision was made, he contacted the Gormley office and arranged a meeting between Olivia and the film's producer Harry Saltzman, the man responsible for the James Bond films.

The meeting went well, according to Welch, and before they left that office, Olivia had been offered the part.

Instead of being introduced to the world via a television series, as with The Monkees, *Toomorrow* were to be launched through the movie media. A press release stated: 'The Kirschner/Saltzman Management clearly believes The Monkees story is about to be rewritten all over again, only bigger!' An album would also be issued on RCA Records, and that, they said, would only be the start! Olivia agreed to become a part of *Toomorrow* and was put on an immediate retainer of ten thousand pounds a year.

The story revolves around four students: Olivia, Ben, Vic and Karl, who are attending London's School of Arts. They perform together as a group – Toomorrow – as well as sharing a house together in Chelsea. John Williams is an alien disguised as a human being, who has been living on Earth for centuries. To normal humans his present occupation has attracted no undue attention. But John is unhappy. He feels he is wasted, until a visiting alien spacecraft provides him with a new challenge. An interesting and powerful vibration has been discovered on Earth and become known to the alien's Galactic Control. As a serious concern in outer-space is a deterioration of sound, this new-found vibration proved invaluable to their needs, and Williams is given the job of tracking down its source. He eventually tracks it to a tonaliser, a strangely designed amplifier, built by Vic, a member of Toomorrow.

After approaching the group, Williams offers the group the chance to rehearse at his Hampstead home. After just one session, a beam whisks them up to a waiting spacecraft. Complete with instruments and Vic's tonaliser, Toomorrow are informed that they are to educate the aliens. For Toomorrow, though, the environment was all wrong, something the aliens soon came to realise, and they allow the group to escape back to Earth.

Over the ensuing months, whilst the film was being completed, Olivia (accompanied by Rona) spent the time jetting back and forth to the United States. The *Sydney Herald* newspaper of November 1969 carried the headline from New York: 'AUSTRALIAN GIRL TO STAR IN $5 MILLION MOVIE!' – 'A pretty Australian singer has been chosen to star in a $5 million film produced by the man who discovered The Monkees. That girl is Olivia Newton-John of Melbourne. "I'm so excited I could burst!" says Miss Newton-John. Asked whether she wanted to return to Australia, she replied, "Not just yet, this is too groovy!"'

The film was finally given a special preview screening in New York, where great things had been expected, considering how much it had cost to make. But it was a major disappointment. Welch considered the film to be a disgrace, with forgettable numbers penned by a group of unknowns who had recently signed with Kirschner's publishing company.

The venture is something Olivia tended to gloss over for many years to come, claiming it as 'an experience I would sooner forget'. Although in later interviews she would talk of the film saying: 'Now [in the Nineties] it would probably make for one of those cult sci-fi film statuses.'

Toomorrow, the group, made one album and released two singles, and the whole thing fell apart. Olivia, on the other hand, lost nothing from the venture. She came out of it with a lot of money and a career on which to build.

PART TWO

If white bread could sing – it would sound like Olivia Newton-John!

Bette Midler

Moving On...

With the Swinging Sixties behind her, and a disastrous film debut firmly buried – the film's producer, Harry Saltzman, later claimed: 'It will never be screened again during my lifetime!' – the dawning of the new decade looked uncertain.

The relationship with Bruce Welch was on rocky ground, having separated once and then got back together again, Olivia decided to take a break and go back to Australia to spend time with her family. During her time in England, her father Bryn had remarried and was now living in Newcastle, New South Wales. Rona had also separated and divorced from Brian Goldsmith, another divorce which had an everlasting effect on Livvy's views on marriage.

Her visit brought a welcome return to Australian television, when she hosted her own variety special – Lovely Livvy for Melbourne's Channel 9 network. Once again she was teamed with her old singing partner, Pat Carroll, who, with Olivia's encouragement, had met and married former guitarist with The Strangers, John Farrar. Another special occasion taking place during the autumn of 1970 was the eagerly awaited opening of the Sydney Opera House. Situated on the famous city harbour, Olivia was a special guest at the opening.

Once back in England, Olivia resumed her relationship with Bruce and plans were underway to go into the studio to record a duet with Cliff Richard, which would prove to be a first for him. Having started his illustrious recording career in 1958, his recording success was unparalleled in the British charts and he had never before shared lead vocals on any record.

'Don't Move Away'[1] was composed by Valerie Avon and Harold Spiro and the session took place at Abbey Road's studio 2 on November 16th, 1970 with Cliff's long-time producer, Norrie Paramor, at the helm. The song was eventually issued in February 1971 as the flip-side to his single 'Sunny Honey Girl'.

By the beginning of 1971, Olivia had been signed to Festival International Records British label, Pye International. Bruce Welch and fellow Shadows guitarist John Farrar, (who had arrived in England in the late Sixties after the break-up of his former Australian band The Strangers, and joined The Shadows) had taken the helm as co-producers of her debut single with the label, which was to be a cover version of Bob Dylan's 'If Not For You', in March 1971.

The early part of the year was spent in the recording studio and a guest appearance on Cliff's popular BBC television show, *It's Cliff Richard*, was planned. 'Olivia was pencilled in to make one show, but our voices worked so well together she stayed for the whole season!' recalls Cliff.

---

[1]The song was eventually issued on CD for the first time in Britain on the album *Cliff Richard – 1970s* by EMI Records in 1999.

With This Ring, I Thee Wed...

The series featured other 'regulars' Una Stubbs and Tim Brooke-Taylor. Amid the music they also featured comedy sketches; one of which was a wedding sequence with Livvy and Cliff as bride and groom – sparking press rumours that they were now an 'item'. 'We were never anything more than friends,' quoted Cliff during an interview on British television in 1997. (Although, a few years later, both Cliff and Olivia would get their revenge on the press by taking part in a telephone hoax to London's Capital Radio – phoning the live request line asking for songs to be played for each other! It later turned out that it was merely Cliff and Livvy trying to sort out a disagreement they were having over a particular song. To resolve the argument, they rang the station and asked them to play the tune – hence, listeners questioning why they were together at that time of night.) Olivia's appearances gave her the opportunity to promote her releases as 'If Not For You' sailed into the British top ten. The song, with its folk/songbird style also scored in Australia and the United States where it peaked at number twenty-five in Billboard's Hot 100. An amazing feat considering she had never been seen on American television! The track also found its way to the top spot on Billboard's Adult Contemporary chart.

In September of that year came the eagerly awaited release of her first self-titled album, a twelve selection compilation featuring 'If Not For You' and Olivia's second single 'Love Song', which the previous year had been a big success for the song's composer Lesley Duncan, although Olivia's version failed to make any impression on the charts.

The album contained a series of cover versions of late Sixties classics: Kris Kristofferson's 'Me and Bobby McGee' and 'Help Me Make it Through the Night', David Gates's haunting melody 'If', which had gone to number one in 1970 for television's *Kojak*, Telly Savalas, and also included Gordon Lightfoot's standard 'If You Could Read My Mind'.

Olivia Newton-John the album, was released in October to mixed reviews. 'Bland and lacking emotion,' wrote the *New Musical Express*. 'A large proportion of the buying public, say in the thirteen to twenty-five age bracket, don't want to know about her. They have established an "anti-Olivia" mechanism in their minds.' Compared to *Melody Maker* magazine who raved: 'We need a bit of glamour around, and it is good to see Olivia breaking through, albeit with a Dylan song.' Olivia's voice possessed a breathy quality which made her performance unique amongst other singers of the early Seventies, and although restricting on a higher vocal register, 'she handled the majority of the songs with ease,' concluded *Melody Maker*.

'Banks of the Ohio' was the third release from her debut album in October. A traditional folk song originally associated with Sixties activist songstress Joan Baez, whom Olivia lists as being a major influence in her early career. As a single it worked extremely well, (despite reviewer Bob Edmands's quip, 'She sings about someone being shot with such flatness in her voice, she might well have been auditioning for the talking clock') going straight into the British top ten and selling in excess of quarter of a million copies, earning a British silver disc award, and also giving Olivia her first number one in her adopted home, Australia, where it achieved gold disc status.

By the end of 1971, Olivia had achieved two top ten British singles, and her debut album had sold fairly well despite not charting. She had also been voted Top Girl Singer in the yearly poll held by *Record Mirror* magazine.

She started the new year on a high; 'Banks of the Ohio' was still floating in the charts and a successful regular slot with Cliff Richard continued. Her next single release came in the form of George Harrison's 'What is Life', with its slightly harder edged arrangement and heavy electric rhythm guitar, it showed Britain's record-buying public that there was more to the songbird style than had first been witnessed. Featuring a who's who of British rock: John Farrar and Kevin Peek (Sky) on guitar, Brian Bennett and Trevor Spencer (Tarney and Spencer) on percussion and Alan Tarney (also of Tarney and Spencer) on bass, the single went straight to number sixteen in the charts.

Not only was Olivia's recording career thriving, but she was also taking a more active role on the cabaret circuit. In February 1972 she was invited to appear as special guest with 'Mr Love' himself – Sacha Distel, whose West End revue *Paris to Piccadilly* was opening at the Piccadilly Theatre on April 12th. The pair worked so well together on stage that once again the press linked Olivia and her co-star romantically, a situation that would eventually be claimed as the main reason behind her split from Bruce Welch later in the year. 'My private life isn't something I really want to talk about,' says Olivia, 'but we were both young and, at the time, both our careers were heading in different directions.'

Yet another cover version was chosen to be Olivia's fifth single for Festival Records. 'Just a Little Too Much', which had been a top ten hit for the song's composer Rick Nelson in the Fifties, was released in August. It failed to catch the public's imagination, and when her second album – *Olivia* – was issued in October, it too fell short of 'projected sales' figures. Again, it was recorded with an array of music's top musicians and composers, and included Olivia's first attempt at writing. 'Changes' tells the story of a divorced couple and the effect their relationship is having on their son – reflections of Livvy's own childhood emotions?

'That song was written at a time in my life when there were a lot of changes going on around me,' explains Olivia. 'It's about divorce and how it affects children and one party still loving the other one and not being able to do anything about it.

'John [Farrar] had been teaching me to play guitar, and I wrote the song in about ten minutes. I'd never written a song before, so for me it was a big thing. I was appearing at the Palladium with Cliff at the time, and I remember dashing into his dressing room saying – I've written this song and I've got to play it to you now before I lose confidence and you can tell me if it's dreadful or not! I was shaking like a leaf, but one of my girlfriends burst into tears, so I figured I'd done the right thing.'

The album received mixed reviews, as with Tony Stewart of the *New Musical Express*, who wrote: 'An album for an artist like Olivia Newton-John means a showcase. She has to show off, let people in on her talents and capabilities.' He continued, 'Her version of David Gates's "Everything I Own", with acoustic guitar and sprinkling piano, is sensitive and refreshing.' He seemed less impressed with the cover version of Gerry Rafferty's 'Mary Skeffington', suggesting that her change of pace on the arrangement lost a lot of the 'aesthetic values of the lyrics'.

Despite flagging record sales, Olivia was invited to be part of the International Music Festival held in Tokyo, Japan. Little did she know at that point that her career in the Far East would escalate into one of the most influential in their history. She ended the year by being voted 'Britain's Favourite Girl Singer' for the second year running by readers of *Record Mirror* magazine.

The highlight of the year must have been her trip to Denmark, where she co-starred with Cliff Richard in a film entitled *The Case*. It also featured Tim Brooke-Taylor and the comedy was based around a mysterious suitcase which Cliff is desperate to dispose of, but can't! During the ensuing storyline, we see and hear Olivia performing live versions of 'Banks of the Ohio' and 'Just a Little Too Much', as well as a duet with Cliff – 'Close to You'.

In August, Olivia flew out to the Far East on a four week concert tour as support act to Cliff Richard. The last time they had travelled overseas together, Olivia was singing backing vocals with Pat Carroll in 1968, but this time she would be performing in her own right. The tour would be visiting Indonesia, Hong Kong and Japan. Projected dates in Singapore and South Korea were cancelled, because local authorities objected to Cliff's long hair, which he refused to have cut!

They arrived back in Britain on September 26th, Olivia's twenty-fourth birthday, and there followed a twenty-three venue tour of Britain, commencing on October 18th.

Country Roads, Take Me Home...

Olivia's music to date had been largely categorised as folk, but her next single was geared more towards country and western, and was to become something of a 'theme song'. In 1971, John Denver had scored a top ten hit in Billboard's Hot 100 with his self-penned song 'Take Me Home Country Roads', but it was Olivia's rendition, issued in November 1972, that had the biggest impact in Britain. Denver was in awe: 'Have you heard her version? The intro comes off like gangbusters!' A compliment for Livvy: the introduction was her idea.

Even though the single was released in November 1972, it didn't actually make an appearance in the British charts until well into February 1973. It went on to hit number thirteen and spend a total of fifteen weeks in the chart. It became synonymous with Olivia, and wherever she appeared, audiences called for her to sing it!

With Olivia back in the charts again, and her television appearances sill happening on a regular basis, it helped to take the pressures away from her split with Bruce; who, so affected by the separation, was said to have attempted suicide.

Work on her third and final album for Pye International began in the summer of 1973, with John Farrar as sole producer. The first single release was 'Let Me Be There', a country-style song written by ex-Shadow guitarist, John Rostill. Despite its catchy arrangement and vocals, the single failed to chart in Britain. In the United States, however, the story was different. Two years earlier, 'If Not For You' had charted for seventeen weeks, peaking at number twenty-five; but with 'Let Me Be There', American listeners took her to heart, sending the disc to number six in the charts!

On the strength of this, Olivia was invited to appear on *The Dean Martin Show*, a high television ratings winner of the early Seventies.

'He rarely came to rehearsals,' recalls Olivia. 'He just comes in when everything's set up. He's so professional!' There were mixed reviews of her appearance: 'The singing milkshake!', 'The singing air hostess!'; and the one that Olivia found concerning – 'If white bread could sing, it would sound like Olivia Newton-John!' The public didn't agree; and neither did the Academy of Country Music, who voted her 'Most Promising Female Vocalist' of 1973 along with her Grammy for 'Best Female Singer – Country category'.

During her promotional tour of the States, Olivia met and became friends with fellow Aussies Helen Reddy and Jeff Wald, who made the point that if Livvy wanted to be a success in America, then she had to be living there!

Olivia took a holiday in the south of France after America, partly to get over the arduous touring; but also to put the break-up of her engagement to Bruce Welch behind her. Whilst relaxing on a friend's yacht in St Tropez, Olivia met and fell for Lee Kramer, a debonair, good-looking English businessman who was eventually to take over the role of manager from Peter Gormley.

In December, MCA records in America released the album version of 'Let Me Be There', a compilation of ten songs, which featured various tracks from her first two British albums along with the title track. Reviews were good, *Record World* magazine wrote: 'This is the kind of music that will take you back in time and soothe your mind. Olivia's style is modern, yet the nostalgia shines through...'. Although it only reached number fifty-four on the Billboard chart and only stayed there for twenty weeks, it was certified gold, with sales in excess of five hundred thousand copies.

Battle of Waterloo...

The new year brought with it many changes: Lee Kramer was now Olivia's acting manager, she had signed with EMI Records in Britain and she had been chosen to represent the United Kingdom in the forthcoming Eurovision Song Contest. Her next studio album, *Music Makes My Day*, was due for release in late February. It was to be her last with Pye International.

As an album it featured twelve songs (and cover photographs taken by world-renowned photographer Patrick Litchfield), including her top twenty hit 'Take Me Home Country Roads' and 'Let Me Be There'. It also carried a cover version of Kiki Dee's chart hit 'Amoureuse' and 'Rosewater', Olivia's self-composed tale of lost love. Fred Dellar of the UK's *New Musical Express* wrote: 'Okay, so it's not heavy! But you'd have to be a real bigot not to admit this is a damn fine album.' He went on to say, '"Being on the Losing End" deserves a Grammy all on its own; and her cover version of the Flett-Fletcher ballad "Leaving" finds Livvy getting inside the song and not being merely superficial.' It entered the charts in March, for three weeks, peaking at number thirty-seven.

By this time, preparations were well under way for her Eurovision entry. BBC television's *Clunk! Click!*, hosted by veteran disc jockey Jimmy Savile, had featured Olivia performing six songs, all of which were in the running as 'Song for Europe 1974'. It was the viewers' vote that would choose the winning song, which went to Valerie Avon and Harold Spiro's 'Long Live Love' (the same writers who had been responsible for Olivia's 1971 duet with Cliff).

Needless to say Olivia wasn't all that impressed, saying she would have preferred a ballad; but it was the viewers' choice. The yearly event was to be held at the Royal Pavilion, Brighton, where Olivia appeared wearing a pastel-blue, flowing butterfly dress. After what seemed a 'lack-lustre' performance: 'I don't think I sang it all that well!' remembers Olivia, the song finally came joint fourth, after 'Waterloo' swept the boards for Sweden's foursome ABBA. The winning group, having been a hit in their homeland for sometime, went on to become the most successful Eurovision winners in history, and didn't become firm friends with Olivia until 1978 when they made a guest appearance on her American television special 'Olivia'. Their friendship finally cemented when Olivia signed with their self-titled record label, Polar, for distribution of her records across Scandinavia. Many of Britain's music sceptics predicted Olivia's failure at the Eurovision as 'the demise of Olivia's career'. In a sense it was true, as regards her British career anyway. (She wouldn't make another appearance in the UK charts until June 1977.) As for the other side of the Atlantic, her American career was gaining pace.

'Long Live Love' the single, went into the British charts to number eleven, and an album of the same name (her first with the new label EMI) was issued in June, spending only two weeks in the chart at number forty. When it was released in South Africa a month later, it was initially banned! Until, that is, two of its tracks were omitted; due to Apartheid laws at that time, lyrics in the songs 'Country Girl' and 'Free the People' were seen as inappropriate. The songs were replaced with 'Let Me Be There' and 'If You Love Me (Let Me Know)' respectively.

The album also contained the Peter Allen composition 'I Honestly Love You'; which MCA records had no plans to release as a single, thinking it too slow. However, when the song was picked up by radio airplay, there was a public demand for it, and so MCA and EMI decided the single would be released simultaneously in October. Although, on home ground it stopped at number twenty-two, in the United States it shot straight to number one, becoming her third gold-selling single in eighteen months following 'Let Me Be There' and 'If You Love Me (Let Me Know)', the latter also being her first number one in their country charts.

'If You Love Me' was another country-style song written by John Rostill, who had penned Olivia's American hit the previous year – 'Let Me Be There'. Unfortunately, he wasn't to witness the results of his work, he died before either song was released.

America Calling...

Following Helen Reddy's advice, and her success over the previous two years, Olivia and Lee Kramer decided to make the move to Los Angeles, where they set up home on a ranch in the Malibu hills. It wasn't long before Livvy had surrounded herself with a menagerie of waifs and strays: seven horses, six dogs and numerous cats.

Making the move to California had been an important step. The single 'I Honestly Love You' had spent two weeks at the number one spot and the album – *If You Love Me (Let Me Know)* (again, featuring a selection of tracks from two UK albums *Music Makes My Day* and *Long Live Love*) had gone straight to the top of the album charts, achieving gold sales within weeks of its release.

'When I recorded "I Honestly Love You" it was in one take,' says Olivia. 'The song really moved me. The lyrics grabbed me from the first time I heard it. I couldn't believe I'd found it and that no one else had done it!'

Within twelve months of arriving in the States, Olivia was to receive over twenty awards for her music, including two more Grammys for the song 'I Honestly Love You' – 'Record of the Year' and 'Best Pop Performance – Female' – but the most controversial award she received was 'Female Vocalist of the Year' from the Country Music Association. Die-hard country veterans were livid that an 'outsider' could come in and win 'their' award. 'We don't want somebody out of another field coming in here and taking away what we've worked so hard for,' said Johnny Paycheck.

Not all were pessimistic; Loretta Lynn backed Olivia saying, 'It's always good to see someone new enter the scene. I've won several awards in Britain and don't feel the least bit resentful towards Olivia's American success.' Stella Parton (younger sister to Dolly, who had been one of the protesters) paid tribute to Olivia in song. 'An Ode to Olivia' appeared as the flip-side to one of her 1975 single releases. Whilst all this acrimony was going on, Olivia was totally unawares, touring the West Coast on a dusty old greyhound bus.

'I've never claimed to be a country singer,' she said on hearing the news. 'To call yourself that, you would have to be born into that background. I simply love country music; and since the records have also sold well outside of the country audience, it seems to me that we're broadening the acceptance for country music. I wasn't out to do anybody out of an award.' Since that situation arose, the borders between country and pop have become more relaxed, allowing for what became known as 'cross-over'. 'Music has to expand,' said Olivia. 'You can't keep it in a bag. You've got to open it out.'

Although now living in the States, Olivia was still working on her British career, flying back to London to film a series of four musical specials for the BBC, titled *Moods of Love*. Each thirty-minute show featured songs of love and poetry readings by selected guests, who included Christopher Casanove, Peter Gilmore, and Neil Sedaka with whom Olivia performed in the opening show. She introduced her first guest with: 'He has introduced me so many times in the past, now it's my turn...' for old friend Cliff Richard. Despite top name guests, the BBC failed to give the show a prime time slot, opting for a late evening airing and depriving it of healthy viewing figures.

Work also began on her next studio album at EMI's Abbey Road studios in London, where the label had also decided to issue a compilation of her earlier hits in the form of *First Impressions*, in time for the Christmas market. The collection included all her UK singles to date, along with a sprinkling of selected standards such as 'Amoureuse' and 'Music Makes My Day'. 'The queen of easy listening trips lightly through a selection of hers and other people's greatest hits,' wrote *Melody Maker*. 'The one thing about Miss Newton-John's brand of MOR, is that you can listen to both sides of almost identical tracks without it sending you running for a sledgehammer.' Although a comparison of Olivia's rendition of the Kiki Dee hit 'Amoureuse' was – 'She unfortunately doesn't have the same depth or range of feeling.'

Queen of Mellow...

Back in England, under the continued guidance of Lee Kramer (as manager) and John Farrar (as producer), Olivia began work on what was to be her fifth studio album. *Have You Never Been Mellow* featured eleven tracks, including the title song by John Farrar, along with two songs by John Denver – 'Goodbye Again' and 'Follow Me' – and Olivia's cover of 'The Air That I Breathe', the song that had been a hit for The Hollies earlier in the year.

The title single entered the American charts in January like a bullet – straight in at number sixty-four and taking only six weeks to reach the top spot, and achieving gold disc sales after only one week at number one. But it was the second single release that would leave the audiences crying for more.

'Please Mr Please' was penned by ex-lover Bruce Welch and John Rostill, and is reported to be Welch's reaction to his relationship with Olivia. Despite recording the song himself, it would, ironically, be Olivia who took it to the top of the charts in 1975, and Olivia who was awarded the 'Country Music Award' by the American Society of Composers, Authors and Publishers (ASCAP).

'I'm sure everyone has a particular song with the person they are in love with at the time. If you hear that song again, even if it's five or ten years later, it will bring back a memory,' she said of her latest American hit. 'Music is a great one for memories. I think that song really hits home.

It must have hit home to a lot of people… it certainly did to me!'

1975 was a very busy year for Olivia, flying back to the States for the album's release, and to co-host the 'American Music Awards' with Glen Campbell and Aretha Franklin, and also preparing for a national tour. The album went straight to number one, her second in a row, and third to achieve gold sales. Whilst hosting the awards ceremony, Olivia performed, for the first time, a montage of her hits to a live audience and also picked up three awards for 'Favourite Female Vocalist' in both the Country and Rock/Pop categories, and 'Favourite Rock/Pop Album' for *Have You Never Been Mellow*.

Having scored in England with 'Take Me Home Country Roads' in 1973, and recording two of his songs on her latest album; John Denver invited Olivia to record a duet with him to appear on his 1975 album *Windsong*. The track was called 'Fly Away', a country-style love song which went to number thirteen on Billboard's Hot 100. Denver was reportedly so impressed with Olivia, that he said: 'If she ever agreed to marry me, I will make her my "first lady" of the United States Government!'

'John rang me and said that he'd written this song,' says Olivia of the duet. 'And he would love for me to record it with him. I was very honoured because I had been a big fan for so long and I had recorded some of his songs.'

The highlight of her year, though, must have been during the last two weeks of August, when she appeared at the Iowa and Minnesota State Fairs. Attracting a capacity crowd of over thirteen thousand people, it proved to be one of the highest attended appearances in the fairs' history. Appearing with Olivia were local band This Oneness, who had been supporting her since 1973. Having opened the show with her usual array of hit songs – 'Let Me Be There' and 'If Not For You', she then went into a rousing version of The Beatles' 'Honey Pie', with its opening line about being a working girl from North England who is now finding success in the USA immediately striking a chord with her American fans. Their approval was shown by a standing ovation!

Olivia's acceptance on the American scene was a far cry from her early days in England, where jeans and shirt would definitely not have been approved of. 'Back in England, I had to be the nice girl-next-door; wearing the nice frilly dresses because of the image I had, that's what people expected of me,' she says. 'In America, my image is completely different. I'm able to be more myself. I not only have different songs, I look different too.'

A second album for the year was issued in October. *Clearly Love* was the first Olivia Newton-John album to be released featuring a gatefold sleeve with lyrics inside. Once again she gained sales of over five hundred thousand copies, achieving gold status in the USA, with the single 'Something Better to Do' going straight to number thirteen in October, Olivia's assault on the American market continued.

A Day in the Life of...

It wasn't just in her music that Olivia was moving forward. Having read and been impressed by the autobiography of Fifties songstress and movie star Doris Day, both Olivia and Lee Kramer decided to try and obtain the movie rights to the book. Kramer believed it would be the ideal project to prove to the world that there was more to Olivia Newton-John than just 'a voice' and hopefully put her 'bad experience' with Toomorrow to bed.

'I've always loved Doris Day,' explains Olivia. 'In some ways, people compare me to her, but it's not a good comparison because as an actress and a movie personality, I have yet to prove myself.' Ms Day was to reject the idea, saying she didn't want her story making into a movie. Preferring to keep her private life private was something Olivia understood perfectly.

Olivia finished the year back home in Australia, where she spent Christmas with her family and also found time to film a television special for the American market with fellow 'country artist' Glen Campbell. *Down Home, Down Under* was filmed in the Melbourne area, and gave an idea of how an Australian Christmas is spent compared to those of the Northern Hemisphere.

Despite the obvious lull in her British and European career, there seemed nothing she could do wrong in the United States. In the two years since arriving in Los Angeles, Olivia had scored with seven charting singles, five of which were top ten and two of those made it to the number one spot! All five were also certified gold discs. She had achieved cumulative sales of over twenty million in just over four years with MCA records in America alone, in both the singles and albums charts, and 1976 looked set to continue the trend.

Work had already started on her next studio album at EMI studios in London. The title track, 'Come on Over', had been composed especially for Olivia by Barry and Robin Gibb and was to be the first single release in March. The album also featured a cover version of Dolly Parton's 1974 chart-topper 'Jolene', the song that would really stamp Olivia's name on the Japanese music charts. She had first scored in 1973 with 'Let Me Be There', but it was with 'Jolene', three years later, that she would achieve her first number one in the Far East.

The album also contained versions of 'The Long and Winding Road' (a Lennon and McCartney classic) and the Greg Benson chart-topper 'Don't Throw it All Away'. It was her most country-orientated album so far, with 'Jolene', 'Come on Over', John Farrar's 'It'll Be Me' and 'Small Talk and Pride', all being in a country vein. As a collection it was well received on the American market, going to number thirteen on the album chart and gaining a gold disc (her fifth album in a row to do so!).

Having been a ratings winner the previous year, Olivia was invited back by NBC to host the 1976 'American Music Awards', performing live once again and also paying a vocal tribute to one of America's premiere songwriters, Irving Berlin. However, she only walked away with one award this year – 'Favourite Female Vocalist – Pop/Rock'.

A popular vehicle for performers in the States was to have their own television show or special. Barbra Streisand, whom Olivia had tied with for the 'People's Choice Award' for 'Favourite Female Vocalist' in 1974, had achieved top-rated shows in the Sixties with her specials 'My Name is Barbra' and 'Color Me Barbra', and Olivia had been approached with a similar idea. Olivia was unsure, she was worried about becoming over-exposed, as had been the case with 'Sonny and Cher', whose successful TV show all but killed their careers and marriage. A one-off show was agreed, and in the summer of 1976, 'A Special Olivia Newton-John' aired to rave reviews.

The show featured guests: TV gossip columnist Rona Barrett; 'Six Million Dollar Man' Lee Majors; 'Wonder Woman' Lynda Carter; 'Happy Days' Ron Howard and Tom Bosley; and a character cameo by Elliot Gould, dressed in evening suit, wielding cane and dancing shoes, performing 'Let's Call the Whole Thing Off' as a kind of audition piece to get on the show. It proved to be a winning formula, sending the show into the top ten ratings for that week.

Nashville, Tennessee...

For the first time in her recording career, Olivia ventured overseas to work on her next album. With John Farrar again at the helm and following the controversy two years earlier regarding her CMA win, it seemed appropriate to pick Nashville to record tracks for *Don't Stop Believin'*. Olivia felt this move would help to lay to rest any bad feelings from the past, and also the best musicians were to be found there.

The album was released by MCA in November, going straight into Billboard's Top Thirty and gaining a gold disc soon after. In December the international hit single 'Sam' was released. Originally written by Hank Marvin and Don Black as the theme tune to one of Harlech Television's (Wales) new soap operas, the show never came off, and John Farrar eventually put lyrics to the melody and it went on to become one of Olivia's best known international records. Only just making Billboard's top twenty, the song put Olivia back into the UK top ten (after a three year absence from our charts). The reason for this, Olivia believes, was the lyrical content: 'The words seemed typically British; they seemed to associate with it.'

Despite the obvious lull in her American singles chart entries, since 'Please Mr Please' hit the top ten in July 1975, Olivia had only made one appearance in the top twenty in the last eighteen months, although having issued six singles, all of which bubbled just outside the top thirty.

'Sam' peaked at number twenty in March 1977, as work began on her next studio album.

As a result of her number one single 'Jolene' in Japan earlier in the year, it was only natural that a concert tour should follow. Dates were planned for November and December, selling out in each major city. The Japanese had taken Olivia's music to their hearts just as sincerely as her American fans had. Before her departure, Olivia read of the Japanese fishermen's senseless slaughtering of innocent marine life, in particular a school of dolphins which lived off the coast of Japan. This incensed her, and she threatened to cancel the tour unless the Japanese government could assure her that they would stop any future killings. She even went as far as to donate money to help find alternative methods; however, because of legal details she was forced to carry out the contracted tour dates.

Two dates in Osaka (on December 2nd and 3rd) were filmed for television and were later given a vinyl release under the title *Love Performance – Olivia Live in Japan!* on EMI records in the Far East only.

Making it Easy...

Making a Good Thing Better was to be Olivia's first attempt at an album aimed purely at the 'Easy Listening' market in 1977. The title track, by Peter Wingfield, featured a more mature sound from Olivia, along with other cover versions of 'Ring of Fire' and Seventies pop brothers the Alessi's 'Sad Songs'. The year's biggest hit song, from the Andrew Lloyd-Webber stage show *Evita*, was 'Don't Cry for Me Argentina', the one track Olivia was eager to record, in the hope that it might put an end to the 'cute' and 'bland' image she was said to have portrayed for so long.

'The pictures on the cover are almost worth the price of the album alone,' wrote Robin Smith in his review for Britain's *Record Mirror*. 'The title track is an average song turned into a speciality, her voice sounding like twelve vestal virgins; and "Don't Cry for Me Argentina" even betters Julie Covington's [who had made it to number one in the British singles chart that year with the same song].'

The album entered both the UK and USA charts, but was the first not to go gold in America. A sign that maybe her temporary departure from country music wasn't quite what her American fans had expected. The critics were very favourable; a US rock reporter commented: 'On "Slow Dancing" you close your eyes and slide out of your seat as her voice trickles everywhere, warming you from head to toe in all the right places, and the tearful quality in her voice is used to best effect on "Cooling Down".'

With a concert tour of America planned for later in the year, there was just time for a flying visit to Britain to record a special for the BBC and also to appear, at Her Majesty's request, at the Royal Command Performance to commemorate the Queen's Silver Jubilee, to be held in the grounds of Windsor Royal Park. During a BBC radio interview Olivia spoke of her excitement, 'It will be the first time that I've sang in front of the Queen. It's an honour, so I am really looking forward to it.'

But it was back in America that things were really working for Olivia. Rehearsals for her national tour had started along with the release of her first *Greatest Hits* collection, which included all her major charting singles from 1971 to 1976. It was well received in the US charts, going to number thirteen and gaining platinum sales (her first album to do so), and also became her first British top twenty entry, despite the critics' choice words: 'Olivia Newton-John offers the cosiest form of alienation around,' wrote Bob Edmands of the *New Musical Express*. 'Her voice is so lacking in emotion, she makes Lou Reed sound hysterical!' Her British critics have always had their daggers drawn where Olivia was concerned.

Her so-called 'image' is something that she never set out to create. She has always chosen songs that cover a wide spectrum of styles, whether it be folk, country or pop. 'Bland' has been one adjective used to describe her style. 'I don't think I'm all that bland,' she says. 'Maybe it comes from the music I sing. Sometimes I find it hard to enjoy a genuine compliment because of the practical nature instilled in me by my mother.'

Olivia's private life was also going through a tough period at this point. Her tempestuous relationship with Lee Kramer had reached the point of no return. Both parties decided to split romantically. 'Breaking up love affairs is as low as you can get,' said Olivia at the time. 'But falling in love is as high. I'm sure both Lee and I went through every emotion possible. When you live with someone for that length of time, it's bound to be difficult.'

Although the couple had separated romantically, they decided to stay together on a professional basis. 'We've been through a lot together, so why not?' said Olivia. 'It seems a shame if after six years together, two people decide never to see each other again. When a person has been a part of your life for so long, has watched you grow and shared so much, isn't it better to be friends?'

Grease is the Word…

Prior to the first night of her current tour, Olivia was invited to a dinner party hosted by friends Helen Reddy and Jeff Wald. Such Hollywood get-togethers had nothing much to do with what was on the menu, but more to do with who was who and what the deal was.

Also attending the Walds' that night was Hollywood film producer Allan Carr, who was in the process of casting a new film version of the 1972 Broadway hit musical *Grease* – a nostalgic look back at teenage middle America in the Fifties, written by Jim Jacobs and Warren Casey. Twenty-seven year old star of television's *Welcome Back Kotter*, John Travolta, fresh from his performance in the soon-to-be-released disco movie *Saturday Night Fever*, had already been cast as the male lead Danny Zuko. Carr was now seeking a leading lady. Star names such as Marie Osmond and Ann-Margaret had been considered, but on meeting Olivia for the first time, Carr knew instantly who he wanted to play Sandy in his screen adaptation of the show.

'We'd never met before attending Helen Reddy's party,' says Carr. 'I thought she was adorable. I asked her if she wanted to do a screen test for *Grease* and she replied, "not particularly!"'

The concert tour was a series of one night shows over a three week period which eventually came to an end in New York City, where Olivia was to make her debut at the prestigious four thousand seat Metropolitan Opera House.

Olivia recalls, 'I was only the second person in my area of singing to appear there and it was my first time in New York, so all in all it was pretty scary and exciting!' Being a perfectionist and highly self-critical, Olivia was more than nervous on opening night, as John Farrar recalls: 'She broke down crying to the point where we didn't think she would be able to go out; but she went on and did the best show she has ever done.'

'My biggest fear was forgetting my lines,' continued Olivia. 'I wrote the words on the palms of my hands. Even the ones I've sang a hundred times.' As a closing night gesture, she presented each member of the audience with a dethorned red rose with a note thanking each and every one for their support throughout her career.

Following the last night of her sell-out tour, Olivia remained in New York to have a meeting with Allan Carr, along with Randall Kleiser (who was making his feature film debut as director), about the prospect of her appearing in the film version of *Grease*. The evening before the meeting, she had spent the night alone in her room at the Sherry Netherlands Hotel, where a sound system had been specially installed so that she could listen, over and over, to the original Broadway cast album of the show.

Olivia had never met Travolta, but had known of his work through his television appearances in *Kotter*, and his previous film with Randall Kleiser – *The Boy in the Plastic Bubble*. The pair met for the first time at Olivia's Malibu home: 'I remember it very well,' explained Olivia to Didi Conn in her book *Frenchy's Grease Scrapbook*, 'I met John for the first time when he came out to my ranch in Malibu. He walked up to the front door, and I thought – Um! He's cute!' Following her previous film encounter six years before, she was determined not to agree to anything she didn't feel capable of handling, and so requested a screen test. Carr agreed, later claiming that her test was 'so perfect,

I could have used it in the film just the way it was.' Olivia signed a contract with Paramount Pictures to the tune of $125,000 plus a percentage of the overall gross to co-star in their $6 million budgeted production.

Filming began in June of 1977 in Los Angeles with a cast list reading like a who's who of Hollywood: Eve Arden, Joan Blondell, Sid Ceasar and a cameo appearance by Frankie Avalon. There were also to be some slight changes to the script. In the original stage production, 'Sandy Dumbrowski' had moved from interstate; but now with Olivia's prominent Australian accent, 'Sandy Olsen' was to have emigrated from Melbourne. Also, the character wasn't initially listed as a dance part, but during dance rehearsals, choreographer Patricia Birch noticed Olivia could move and so the part was worked on and given several dance routines. Along with the original Casey/Jacobs score, four new songs were added to the film's soundtrack. These songs were written by John Farrar and Barry Gibb, and the first of them, 'You're the One That I Want' (a duet with John Travolta) was issued on single in April, closely followed by the album in June. In the original score, the part of Sandy had no big solo number (except the reprise of 'Look at Me, I'm Sandra Dee'), and part of Olivia's agreement to star in the picture was to have a solo song.

'As we went into production, there was no song and no idea where we would put it. It wasn't even on the production schedule,' said director Randal Kleiser to the *Los Angeles Times* in March 1998. 'John Farrar came up with "Hopelessly Devoted to You" halfway through production, but time was running out and we had to figure out where to put the song and how to integrate it into the story. It was one of the last scenes we shot, almost in one take.'

The on-screen chemistry between the two stars was igniting. Olivia quotes Travolta as being 'one of the most generous actors you could work with', following one occasion during filming when John purposely fluffed one of his lines simply because he felt Olivia could 'do better in her close-up' than she had done so far. The close-knit relationship lead to tabloid speculation that the two were having an affair, particularly as Olivia had recently split from long-time lover Lee Kramer. Olivia, who has always guarded her private life with a vengeance, denied that their relationship was anything other than platonic. Although, in a later interview, Travolta was to claim that they did actually have a romantic interlude; despite his having recently lost the love of his life, Diana Hyland, to cancer.

On set, fellow cast member and Malibu neighbour, Didi Conn remembers: 'We were all so jealous because she got to kiss John and she wouldn't tell us what it was like! We were dying!'

Olivia continues, 'I'm sure I was just as naive as Sandy is. Most girls at that age go through similar experiences; but I don't think I was mixed up with quite the same kind of girls though.'

At thirty years of age, it seemed strange for Olivia (along with the rest of the high school cast) to be playing the part of a teenager. Although her manager Lee Kramer had full confidence in her: 'She's a complete woman, with all the normal feelings of an adult – not a child. In this film, she plays an eighteen-year-old, which is quite an accomplishment for someone her age. To go back in time and play demure and innocent and all those other school girl things.'

The one thing about the script that attracted Olivia was the ending, when 'sweet, naive Sandy' decides the only way to get her man is to change her image. Where Sandy #1 becomes Sandy #2 (as Olivia prefers to put it): 'I remember the first day before shooting that scene. I had my hair permed and wore the spandex trousers with high heels and make-up, and walked out on the set with a cigarette in my mouth. Nobody recognised me. It was great! That was the beginning of my sexual liberation.'

Upon the movie's release there were mixed receptions. America's *Blue Print Magazine* wrote: 'This adaptation of the Broadway hit is an exciting, energetic salute to the golden age of rock 'n' roll'. One reviewer wrote that Olivia's performance was 'wet' and 'drippy', despite the fact that she was playing a 'wet and drippy caricature girl'. *New Musical Express* responded with: 'How did they expect a cheerleader to act – smoking a cheroot and cutting balls off with her tongue? What's their idea of a "good" actress?' At its Los Angeles premiere (on June 2nd) at Graumann's Chinese Theatre on Hollywood Boulevard, fans flocked in their thousands to get a glimpse of the two stars arriving in a white, open-top, stretch limousine. A completely different story to their British opening (on September 14th), where the film was honoured with a Royal Premiere. Fans had been gathering outside the Empire Cinema in Leicester Square since early morning; by the time the pair arrived, the waiting hordes were uncontrollable. Police and extra security had to be brought in to usher the stars into the theatre. The following day's tabloid headlines all echoed: '*GREASE* PREMIERE IN LONDON AN EVENT OF RIOT PROPORTION!', and 'THE BIGGEST HAPPENING OF ITS KIND EVER – INCLUDING DAYS OF THE BEATLES!'

Olivia's Hollywood film debut had proved a resounding success. The first single, with Travolta, had topped the world's charts, achieving platinum sales in Britain after a nine week run at the top, closely followed by their second single, 'Summer Nights', which again went straight to number one for a seven week dominance, attaining the duo the acknowledgement as being the 'only double act in the UK charts to achieve their first two single releases go to the top' and 'the longest run at the number one position'. The soundtrack album also topped the worldwide charts, going multi-platinum and spending over two months in pole position. Reviews of the album were good, *Record Mirror* commented: 'I like Olivia's reprise of "Look at Me", she has a lovely voice – precise and clear – but mostly she gets lost in the general production of the tracks.'

Within six months of release, the film would gross over $132 million in the United States alone and a staggering $190 million worldwide. Olivia's career as a singer had made her an international recording star, but *Grease* had introduced her to a whole new legion of fans – the movie goers.

In September, Olivia entered into a legal dispute with MCA Records (her American distributor) claiming that they were 'failing to give her the promotion she warranted'. This was backed by Robert Stigwood (owner of RSO Records, who were sole distributors of the *Grease* sound-track), who, unsuccessfully, tried to buy out Olivia's contract with the label. MCA, in turn, counter-sued for $1 million maintaining that Olivia 'had not fulfilled her obligations with them as an entertainer'. 'We had some kind of litigation. We settled and now we're friends again,' she said in a later interview. 'In the end, it improved things between the record company and myself.'

Her music career continued to flourish, with her only solo offering from the soundtrack – 'Hopelessly Devoted to You' – entering the charts in November, narrowly missing the top of the charts (it peaked at number two for two weeks) in early December. She would also be approached by *Playboy* magazine, offering her a cool $1 million to pose nude for their new year centrefold. Olivia flatly refused, 'disgusted' by the idea.

A Scorching Success...

Having achieved international success with her Hollywood movie debut in *Grease*, Olivia's next recording venture was to be a more adult-orientated project in the form of the album *Totally Hot*. Recording began in Los Angeles in July, and was to feature John Farrar as producer (a role that he has taken throughout the majority of her career), and also composer on several of the tracks.

It was hoped that the album would shatter Olivia's 'squeaky-clean' image completely. The album featured songs written by Farrar, Eric Carmen, Olivia and a questionable cover version of The Spencer Davis Group's 'Gimme Some Lovin'', the track on the collection that fetched the most criticism from reviewers. The first single release came in November with the John Farrar song 'A Little More Love' and the album followed two weeks later to devastating reviews! On the British music scene, the critics were less than favourable, with James Parade of *Record Mirror* writing: '*Totally Hot* rates as the most misleading title ever! In my book, "hot" comes somewhere near "fervent", "lecherous" or "fiery". Well, the only fire here is that seeping from Olivia's eyes in the beautiful picture on the inner sleeve...'

His views were echoed by Julie Burchill of *New Musical Express*: 'She's all face and hair and walk and not much else! This is her umpteenth in a long line of voids, and the content stays much the same...' The one thing they did both agree on was the single: 'The only spark of life is on "A Little More Love".' Despite the criticism, however, the single entered the British top ten, and on the other side of the Atlantic, where they have always been consistently in favour of Livvy's work, both single and album went into the charts, achieving gold and platinum sales respectively.

Two more singles were issued from the album (the title track and 'Deeper Than the Night') both of which fared better in the US market. In Britain, however, a limited edition picture disc version of the album was issued, although a chart placing of only thirty was reached. MCA Records followed this with a limited issue picture disc single of 'Deeper Than the Night' for American fans.

Following the international success of her American movie debut, Olivia embarked on an extensive world tour, which started in the United States in September, moved to Australasia in November and on to Britain for just four dates. The first British dates were at the Manchester Apollo on November 27th and 28th, followed by two appearances at The Rainbow in Finsbury Park, North London, on December 6th and 7th.

The entourage included ten imported musicians, three imported backing vocalists and the back drops from her sell-out shows in Las Vegas. All the international performances were well attended and received, but in England, as had come to be expected, the knives were once again drawn. John Wishart of *Record Mirror* had mixed feelings, saying: 'Clearly Hollywood has turned her head!' He continued, 'I got the distinct impression that Livvy is fed up with her image of reigning MOR queen. The totally hot hype has forced her vocal chords into a brand new key and it sounds godawful!' The one number he mentioned with some praise was 'Jolene' – 'the one that shows her voice off to its best advantage'.

After her opening night in London, Olivia was guest of

honour at a post-gig party held at the Embassy Club. Fellow guests included Britt Ekland, Phil Lynott, ex-Sex Pistols Paul Cook and Steve Jones, and Pete Townshend.

Roll of Honour...

On the wave of Livvy's international superstardom, it seemed the perfect accolade when Australia's premiere recommended her to the British monarchy for an acknowledgement in their New Year's Honours List in recognition of her contribution to entertainment. On New Year's Day 1979 it was announced that Olivia was to be awarded the OBE (Officer of the Order to the British Empire).

'When I first heard the news, I was overwhelmed and rang my office thinking it was a practical joke,' said Olivia. What made the news all the more auspicious was considering that Sixties supergroup The Beatles, who had been recognised in the previous decade, had only got MBEs. Joining her on the list of recipients was television star Gordon Jackson. 'I wasn't nervous until I heard my name called,' recalls Olivia. 'I was the first woman in our set to go; and I was worried I might trip up or forget to curtsey or walk backwards or something.'

Also in January, one of the world's most notable pop groups The Bee Gees, joined forces with UNICEF to put together a live concert to raise funds in aid of the year of the child. The idea was to involve fellow performers, who would give their time freely and donate the proceeds of their individual performances to the cause. The event was to be held at the General Assembly Hall of the United Nations in New York. Big names to be involved included

John Denver, Rod Stewart, Donna Summer, Olivia and Andy Gibb. Olivia contributed one song – 'The Key', along with a duet with Andy Gibb, a cover version of a Gibb brothers track – 'Rest Your Love on Me'. So convincing were the pair in their rendition of the song's lyrics that, off-stage, gossip columnists wrote that there was a relationship between them. Even though, at that time, Andy was heavily in a relationship with television actress Victoria Principal. Andy and Olivia eventually ventured into the recording studio to record a studio version of the song along with another Gibbs-composed track – 'I Can't Help It', which, when issued on single, entered the American top fifteen in the spring of 1980.

In fact, Gibb had fallen in love with and married his childhood sweetheart, Kym, in Sydney in 1976 at the age of eighteen, later becoming a father on January 5th, 1978. The couple eventually divorced five months after the birth of their daughter, Pieter. Having achieved instant international fame (albeit, in the shadow of his famous brothers who formed The Bee Gees), at such an early age, involvement in the world of drugs sent his career and personal life into turmoil for the next ten years. Having made successful comeback attempts, Gibbs's battle with his addiction came to a close on March 10th, 1988, when he died of a drugs related condition at only thirty years of age.

The new year brought forth more surprises, in that Olivia's solo single from the *Grease* soundtrack – 'Hopelessly Devoted to You', was nominated for 'Best Song' in both the 51st Annual Academy of Motion Picture Awards (Oscars) and the 21st Annual Grammy Awards. Olivia performed live on both occasions, but unfortunately lost out on each count to Debbie Boone's 'You Light Up My Life'.

It had been almost two years since *Grease* had begun its first stages of production and Olivia was now looking for something that could possibly follow it. There had been talk of working with Alan Carr on his next project, another musical to be called *Discoland*, but it never got off the ground. The Hollywood press picked up on what they quoted as 'the real reason behind the production's problems', and Carr fuming: 'I've just thrown her [Olivia] off the set of my next $12 million picture because of her excessive demands. Her demands are now what Streisand's were after *Funny Girl*, and she ain't no Streisand!'

Olivia later admitted, 'It never really got beyond the discussion stage.' The film would eventually be made under the new title *Can't Stop the Music*, featuring Seventies pop sensations the Village People.

Flights of Fantasy...

One script that arrived on Olivia's desk that intrigued her was a twenty page outline of a story loosely based on the 1954 musical fantasy *Down to Earth*, which had starred Rita Hayworth. The story revolves around the Greek goddess of music (Terpsichore) and a Broadway producer, who is putting together a musical based on the lives of the eight muses. In the new version, Kira (goddess of dance) is sent to Earth to help a former big-band leader and young artist open a dance venue. 'I knew instantly this was the one,' said Olivia. 'It was a fantasy movie – which had no violence – and that is exactly what I feel everybody needs right now.'

By late 1979, Olivia was back in Hollywood preparing for her second major movie – albeit a remake of a Fifties success story. *Xanadu* had been taken up by Universal Pictures, and cast alongside Olivia was Michael Beck, although the main male lead had yet to be filled. In fact, filming was well underway before it was announced that Forties dance legend, Gene Kelly, had been signed. 'It was extremely hard getting Gene to sign,' says the film's producer Larry Gordon. 'He was very charming, but would only do it on one condition – he wouldn't sing or dance one step.'

Coincidentally, two months before accepting the picture, Olivia had taken up tap dancing lessons, as an outside interest. When Kelly finally accepted and eventually got into the mood of the picture, he gave in and decided to perform in one routine, which he would choreograph. Olivia was more than a little taken back by his change of mind. Having admired her co-star for many years, the prospect of singing and dancing with the legendary Gene Kelly left her in total awe. 'I was very nervous,' recalls Olivia. 'But he was amazing and really patient. He wouldn't let me do anything I didn't feel comfortable with.'

Behind the scenes things were tense to say the least. Writers were being hired and fired, until eventually the film's director, Robert Greenwald, took over as writer; handing out lines in the morning and changing them again later in the day. Michael Beck recalls: 'From the point of view of an actor, with the constant script changes, it was hard to know where your character was heading.'

Amongst the cast though, there seemed to be no hard feelings. 'I enjoyed the atmosphere on set,' recalls Olivia. 'There were a lot of young people and the energy was great.' Gene Kelly was just as impressed with the way things were looking: 'In doing this kind of film, with new music as opposed to the music I am used to [Gershwin and Porter etc;] is a real step ahead for these young people.'

That was compared to filming conditions of the musicals of the Forties and Fifties, when the whole production company were all part of a repertory style organisation, with every member of the team under contract and working together the whole time. Kelly continued, 'We didn't have to search for months on end to get a crew together, like they do these days. I admire the fact that they do it as quickly as they do!'

Larry Gordon, the movie's producer, was full of praise for the cast, saying of Olivia, 'she is the consummate professional. A film star for the future.' He went on to say, 'If I had to create my all-star cast, then Olivia Newton-John would definitely be my leading lady.'

Where there were short-comings in the script, it was

being more than made up for in the music, with the soundtrack featuring songs by John Farrar and Jeff Lynne (of rock group Electric Light Orchestra). Five tracks by ELO would be used over various film sequences, with the title track featuring Olivia on lead vocals; and another set of numbers for Olivia to perform throughout the film. Guest vocal included a duet and impromptu dance number with Gene Kelly (who choreographed the sequence), an amalgamation of the Forties meets the Eighties with The Tubes, and a duet with old friend Cliff Richard.

'When John [Farrar] wrote the duet for the movie, we wanted someone to sing it with me,' says Olivia. 'Someone who was a well-known singer. Cliff had just had his first big hit in the States and I thought – it would be great to have him because he gave me my first break in England. To have him sing with me now would be great!'

'I still find it absolutely a pleasure to sing with Livvy,' said Cliff of the venture. 'To record "Suddenly" with her was a fantastic thrill! It doesn't matter that it didn't go top five in the charts, because sometimes you have to do things that you know are artistically the right thing to do.'

'It was a totally different experience writing for a film,' said Jeff Lynne. 'Compared to going into a studio, where I can record an album and change anything I want as I go along, before I release it. At this point, I have to commit myself totally to what I've recorded and say "here is the finished product, you can use it in the film".'

A release date of early spring 1980 was pencilled in for *Xanadu*, as the successful Seventies drew to a close for Olivia Newton-John OBE.

PART THREE

If you have any preconceived ideas about me in the Eighties, you better hold on to your hats!

Olivia Newton-John

Top: Olivia with Bruce Welch following their engagement announcement in October 1968. © UPPA.

Bottom: The original line-up of the group Toomorrow in 1970. (From left to right) Benny Thomas, Olivia, Chris Slade (who would later be replaced by Karl Chambers for the film) and Vic Cooper. © UPPA.

Top: Olivia with Cliff Richard during their successful union on his BBC TV show in October 1971. © UPPA.
Bottom: Paris to Piccadilly – with Sacha Distel in March 1972. © UPPA.

Top: Putting the finishing touches to her second album in 1972.
© *Express* Newspapers.
Bottom: The most successful movie-musical of all time –
Grease. With John Travolta. © Paramount Pictures.

Top: Receiving the OBE at Buckingham Palace in March 1979. © UPPA.
Bottom: Sporting a new hairstyle for the London premiere of *Xanadu* in September 1980. © UPPA.

Top: Olivia with husband Matt and daughter Chloe on a visit to London in July 1988. © UPPA.

Bottom: With Pat Farrar at the 1990 opening of their Koala Blue Store in South Yarra, Melbourne. © *Herald & Weekly Times.* Melbourne.

Top: Making a welcome return to live performances – appearing with long-time friend Sir Cliff Richard on his 40th Anniversary Tour of Australasia in February 1998. © *Herald and Weekly Times.* Melbourne.

Bottom: A star-studded party following the 20th Anniversary Premiere of *Grease* at London's Empire Cinema, Leicester Square in June 1998. (From Left to right) TV presenter Gloria Hunniford, actress Susan George and Olivia's daughter Chloe Lattanzi. © Richard Mudhar.

A Million Lights are Dancing...

As the new decade began, things were looking decidedly brighter for Olivia. Whilst filming *Xanadu*, she had met and made friends with a dancer from the production, Matt Lattanzi, who at twenty-two was ten years her junior. He had been a temporary leading man whilst Larry Gordon was trying to convince Gene Kelly to sign.

'I thought he was gorgeous!' said Olivia. 'We became good friends first, before we started dating.' At first Olivia was a little dubious about the ten-year age gap, but having established a deep friendship first, that helped the relationship to get started.

Not only did she have a new man in her life, but she had also signed with new management. Lee Kramer had left the fold completely and Olivia was now being represented by his colleague, fellow Australian Roger Davis, who held a list of recognisable clientele, including Cher and Tina Turner. It was Davis who declined joining Ms Turner on a promotional trip to Europe in order to accompany Olivia to her Hollywood premiere of *Xanadu* in May.

A major publicity campaign was put into force for *Xanadu*, with Olivia going before the cameras one more time to make her third special for the US market. *Hollywod Nights* was to be a musical spectacular featuring a cross-section of live concert material with more intimate studio sequences. An array of special guests had been lined up to appear including: Gene Kelly in a song and dance routine 'Making Movies'; Cliff Richard for their soundtrack duet 'Suddenly'; Andy Gibb to promote the release of their single 'I Can't Help It'; Elton John, who accompanied Olivia on piano in a touching rendition of his classic tribute to Marilyn Monroe 'Candle in the Wind'; cameo appearances were also made by Karen Carpenter, Toni Tennille, Peaches, and Tina Turner in a rousing, all-girl teaming of the Eagles' 'Heartache Tonight'. Studio executives were manipulative in their timing for the airing of the special. It was shown as the run-in to the 52nd Annual Academy Awards broadcast, guaranteeing high viewing figures, which the following week proved to have been phenomenal, with *Hollywood Nights* coming in at number four in the ratings.

The film's music was already proving highly successful. In the United States, *Magic* (Olivia's solo) was making a swift ascent in the singles chart; and in Britain, the theme song (featuring Olivia with the Electric Light Orchestra), was starting to move towards the top of the charts. Olivia's statement to the Associated Press read: 'They're a kind of ethereal song, written for the character I play. It's a new style for me, which I like.' But upon the film's release the bubble burst! The critics dismissed the project completely! Ethan Morden in *The Hollywood Musical* commented: 'She has two expressions. She used the miffed one in *Grease*, so in *Xanadu* she uses the impish one.'

This time round the critics appeared to have won, with audiences staying away in their droves. Universal were later to announce that *Xanadu* had been the studio's biggest financial flop to date. Rumour even had it that when the film was screened on an internal American flight, 'passengers were literally trying to leave the plane at thirty-five thousand feet'.

The major failing in the movie was the script; but the

few 'positive' things about the picture were Olivia's costumes throughout and, obviously, the music, which featured a song and dance routine between Olivia and Gene Kelly. 'Whenever You're Away from Me', composed by John Farrar, was in typical Forties big-band style and the sequence was filmed in a large, wall-to-wall mirrored ballroom with Kelly choreographing the routine himself. He wrote of the experience in his autobiography in 1989: 'It was fun working with Olivia and, for that reason alone, I don't regret it; and it's the last time you will ever see me dancing in a movie. So in that respect, I guess *Xanadu* occupies a special place in my career.' On the film itself, he seemed less than impressed: 'I have to admit it was a terrible film. It cost far too much simply because they didn't know how to proceed along economical lines. It could have been made in a third of the time at a third of the cost!'

The film eventually opened in London, with a gala premiere on September 18th at The Plaza Theatre in Piccadilly. Olivia attended sporting a new look. Gone was the trademark shoulder-length blonde hair and in was the new, cropped, feather-cut. She was accompanied by her manager Roger Davis and sister Rona, spending the duration of her stay at London's Inn on the Park. The film was well-received by its first night audience, and a post-premiere party was held at Stringfellow's. But the British press slated the picture, with Felix Barker of the *London Evening News* writing: 'It's the most tasteless, dreadful movie of the decade. Indeed, probably of all time!' During an interview on BBC radio in 1992, Olivia said of the film's failure: 'I kind of got a clue when I found out the director hated music! He was going through a divorce at the time and the scripts were being written and handed out as we went along, so I guess I had a gut feeling!'

The film also met with acrimony when it was due for

release in Australia, where plans had been made for Olivia to make personal appearances to promote the picture. Two weeks before its Sydney Premiere, America's Screen Actors Guild (of which Olivia was now a member – being classified as an actress) called an all-out strike over a pay dispute and Olivia's trip came under threat. Luckily, she was able to make the trip after all – as a singer – to promote the film's soundtrack album and also be honoured by the Mayor of Melbourne. In a crowded Town Square on Swanston Street, he handed Olivia the 'Key to the City' – naming her 'Melbourne's Favourite Daughter'.

A Fine Romance...

The remainder of 1980 was pretty quiet for Olivia. Following her continued assault on the American charts *Magic*, from the *Xanadu* soundtrack, appeared in the 23rd Annual Grammy Awards nominations for 'Best Female Vocal Performance – Pop/Rock'; but proved unsuccessful, for this year anyway.

Her relationship with Matt Lattanzi was slowly developing. Talking on British television in 1995, she remarked, 'First we were friends, then he asked me out, then we split up; but then eventually we got it together.' The ten year age gap obviously proved a stumbling block, for Olivia mainly. 'I used to gravitate towards men who were strong, self-assured and almost arrogant,' she continued. 'But Matt is more relaxed. I was the one who had the hang-up with him being younger than me. He didn't worry – I did. We kept it quiet for a long time. I was afraid it wouldn't work out.'

One question that was constantly asked of Olivia was 'Do you think you will ever marry and have a family of your own?' To which her response had always been 'You have to find someone to marry first! And when I do, I want it to be for life.' Following her parents' divorce and the failing of two marriages for sister Rona (having divorced from Brian Goldsmith, Rona had met Jeff Conway whilst on the movie set of *Grease* and married him in 1979. They divorced in 1985), Olivia was determined to make any union work out for her. One minute she said: 'I've done everything I want to do in my career – a husband and children are the one thing left I would like to do'; and the next – 'I certainly don't need to marry for security and it's not a decision that I take lightly. There's no need to rush into anything – I have plenty of time.'

'Right now, I feel like I'm on a freeway, which is straight and going forward,' Olivia said on *USA Today* in 1980. 'But it has exits, and I can turn on any side road that I want. One exit I could take would lead to my perfect house. Lately I've found myself doodling little pictures of cottages, with white picket fences and white-washed walls and inside I see a happy family with children. But that doesn't mean I want to turn my back on my career. I have a wonderful life. I realise I'm very fortunate.'

Having already appeared at two Royal Command Performances (in 1977 for the Queen's Silver Jubilee and in 1978 for the *Grease* premiere) it was no surprise to read that Olivia was to top the bill at a Royal Charity Concert to be held on May 27th in Sydney, Australia. Her Majesty the Queen and the Duke of Edinburgh were to be the honoured guests at Sydney's Royal Opera House, with television star Bert Newton as compere for the evening. Other well-known Australian celebrities to attend the event included Helen Reddy, Peter Allen and comedian Paul Hogan. Olivia flew in especially for the occasion and played to a warm and welcoming audience. Olivia treated the capacity audience to a medley of hits; the stage was then covered in darkness, bar a spotlight on Olivia. The orchestra started playing the instantly recognisable opening strains of 'Don't Cry for Me Argentina'; and Olivia was backed by a choir of over three hundred voices. Halfway through the song, the darkness was interrupted by a sea of small lights held by each member of the choir. The end of the song prompted a well-deserved standing ovation.

Despite being born in England, Olivia has always regarded Australia as home; and that night was her chance to pay homage to the country that had accepted her with open arms. So popular was the rendition with both the audience and television viewers that Festival Records, her Australian distributor, decided to issue the track as a limited edition single, which made it into the charts for four weeks mid year.

Olivia's work schedule over the past decade had been hectic to say the least. As the new decade got under way she took time to relax and to reflect on where she had been and where her career could go to next. Her relationship with Matt was starting to take shape and she was already looking for new material for her next studio album. There had also been talk of a cinematic reunion with her *Grease* partner, John Travolta, in a sequel. *Grease 2* was well into the discussion stages, but nothing concrete was written. Both John and Olivia turned down any offers to appear, luckily. The film was eventually made starring Maxwell Caulfield (of television's *The Colbys*) and Michelle Pfeiffer (in her cinema debut) in 1982, but proved a financial flop!

By early 1981, Olivia was back in the recording studio, accompanied by long-time friend, composer and producer John Farrar; who has been responsible for her recorded work since the very beginning. Work began on a new collection of songs and with Olivia's new hairstyle came a whole new sound. Farrar appeared as writer/composer on several of the tracks and there also appeared a track penned by Olivia herself – 'The Promise (The Dolphin Song)', a romantic song about dolphins and their relationship with mankind. The song was inspired by an encounter Olivia had had with a dolphin school whilst on holiday in Hawaii. 'I had already started this melody but was having trouble finishing it,' says Olivia. 'Then I went swimming with the dolphins in Hawaii, and the following day the rest of the song was there. I honestly believe they gave it to me.'

The album's title track – 'Physical' – which was composed by fellow Australian Steve Kipner and Terry Shaddick, was actually brought to Olivia's attention by Matt, who encouraged her to record the song. 'At the time, I wasn't in the mood for tender ballads,' says Olivia. 'I wanted peppy stuff because that was the way I was feeling.' *Peppy* was a slight understatement. The album contained ground-breaking titles (musically, for Olivia) such as 'Landslide' (UK top twenty), 'Make a Move on Me' (USA top five) and 'Stranger's Touch', along with a track called 'Carried Away', which had originally been recorded by Barbra Streisand for her 1980 album *Guilty*. Barbra dropped the song and it was later offered to Olivia.

An early autumn date was given for an international release, but at the beginning of September Olivia was in Europe, making a rare live appearance (she hadn't done any live concerts since 1978) in Holland, where she gave the first single release its European premiere. With its 'suggestive' lyrics, Olivia was more than nervous about issuing it on single.

'The week before it went out,' says Olivia, 'I thought about changing my mind and withdrawing it. It was difficult, because this would totally shatter any goody-goody image I may have had in the past!' The single and album were simultaneously released in Britain on October 31st, to mixed reviews.

In America, the single went into the charts like a bullet and within weeks had rocketed to number one, gaining gold sales before the end of the year. In Britain it just scraped into the top ten, where the accompanying video clip was banned by BBC television. Olivia backed up recent comments about the single with, 'As you get older, you get a little more courageous, and you stop worrying what everybody in the world is going to think about you.

You realise not everyone will like you and there will always be people who don't. I think as I get older – I find the world a much more interesting place.'

Let's Get Physical...

Accompanying the album was a long-form video, featuring films for each track. The most controversial of which was the title track, which featured 'scantily clad muscle men'. As the headline appeared in the *Sun*: 'Posing half naked, and towards the end of the song, they are seen pairing off hand in hand to go into the showers!' The lyrical content of the song also prompted certain religious groups across America to 'ban' the track from their airwaves. 'Five years ago, I would have died over a controversy like this,' said Olivia. 'But now, I just think it's foolish of them to take it so seriously.' Olivia's Seventies image had been well and truly updated, and the adverse publicity did the song more good than harm – it was 'Best Selling Single of the Year' on Billboard's chart for both 1981 and 1982!

The video album – which also featured specially filmed segments to 'A Little More Love', 'Magic' and 'Hopelessly Devoted to You' – was released in February 1982 to rave reviews! Britain's *New Musical Express* was highly favourable: '"Physical" taken totally, has to be one of the best pop videos yet marketed.' They went on to commend Olivia with: 'She knows how to move her head and eyes, just how long to hold a stare. She also knows how to walk and dance to the beat of a song.' It is interesting to note that Olivia was the fore-runner where the music video market was concerned. As a promotional ploy in the late Seventies, record companies worked on the idea of individual film clips to help sell a particular single. Olivia, along with director Brian Grant, decided to make a complete set of film clips to accompany all ten tracks of an album, an idea never before considered by any artist or label.

The video sold widely throughout the world, so much so that MCA records decided to release an edited version (featuring specially recorded introductions by Olivia) for television. She opened the television version with: 'These are the Eighties and times change, and people have to change right along with them. Not that you have to throw away everything from the past, just that we have to learn to look at old things in a new way!' A view that she would hold to throughout the coming years as each new year brought a new Olivia. In March 1982, 'Physical' was nominated in two categories at the 25th Annual Grammy Awards – 'Best Performance by a Female – Rock/Pop' and 'Best Video – Long Form', winning in the latter category only. In fact, that category was initiated for the first time that year, especially to honour the 'Physical' video! A Grammy wasn't the only honour bestowed on Olivia in 1982 – to mark her achievement in the recording industry, and success on the American charts, she was given a 'star' on the Hollywood Walk of Fame.

On the strength of the album and video sales, Olivia decided to embark on a sell-out, thirty-two date concert tour of the United States, beginning in August 1982. Rehearsals were due to commence in July, but had to be put on hold when it became obvious that Olivia was being pursued by an over-zealous fan, who had been bombarding her with 'mail' since he saw her in the movie *Xanadu*. This wasn't the first time a fan had tried to get to Olivia (and wouldn't be the last – she would be terrorised by another 'fan' a few years later), and this incident forced her to beef up her already stringent security arrangements. 'Unfortunately it's necessary,' she explained to the *Los Angeles Times*.

'Most fans are well-meaning and caring, but there is that element that may do you harm. Following John Lennon's death, I don't want to take any risks with myself or my friends.'

'The main thing I dislike is having to be protected,' she confessed to British reporter, Charlie Reed. 'I have a full-time guard at my home in Malibu, and on the odd occasion when I have sneaked out to go shopping, I've been told off. I've been in Hollywood for almost ten years now, and have had to be harder and more discerning about the people I can trust.'

Disturbed by the situation, Olivia fled to Australia to spend time with her father until the stalker was apprehended. She spent the time relaxing at her Sydney harbourside penthouse, and even after hearing news of his arrest, Olivia remained in Australia for a further week and attended the world premiere of the Australian film *Phar Lap* with her father.

Once back in Los Angeles, Olivia launched into rehearsals and also put the finishing touches to two new songs she had recorded which were to be included on another compilation of *Greatest Hits*, to be released in conjunction with the tour. The British version of *Olivia's Greatest Hits* was to include twenty hits (compared with the American and Australian versions, which featured only the singles released between 1977 and 1982) from 1971 through 1981, plus two new songs: 'Heart Attack' (from the team who had helped put 'Physical' at the top of the charts) and 'Tied Up'. The concert tour was planned over the following three months and took Olivia to Weber State College, Utah, where twelve months previously she had been banned by local radio stations for the suggestive lyrics on 'Physical'. Ironically, it was these performances, before a record-breaking 135,000 strong crowd, that were recorded for television and later for release on video.

Newton-John has always been renowned for the 'breathiness' of her voice and has always sounded delicate on record: 'her nearly colourless voice being distinguished mainly by the break between a perky chest register and a fragile head voice' (*TV Guide*, USA), but she managed a full ninety minute set with no obvious strain. The reviewer went on to comment: 'Purists may be offended, but pop singers like Miss Newton-John make new styles safe for mass audiences just as they are on the way out. She began her latest single, 'Heart Attack', with punky pogo dancing, sounding a last call for the Seventies new wave.' To round off his views of Olivia's performance he wrote: 'That pop persona threatens to outlast her more progressive experiments', a sign that maybe not all were impressed with the way she was steering her music career.

On previous television airings of live recorded pop concerts TV networks had suffered poor ratings, except in the case of Elvis Presley's late Sixties concerts. Now, the popularity of Olivia Newton-John – Eighties Pop Siren – pushed her concert special to number one in the week's ratings! With its special effects and highly intricate camera work, it went on to outsell all other concerts when issued on video. *Olivia's Greatest Hits*, issued on EMI Records in Britain in October, was well received by the music press and the buying public. It would be her first album to crack the UK top ten (aside from her appearances on the soundtracks for *Grease* and *Xanadu*), *Physical* had just missed, peaking at number eleven in February. The latest compilation went on to spend thirty-eight weeks in the charts, gaining a UK gold disc.

Second Chance...

There were still discussions taking place about Olivia teaming up with John Travolta on another picture, with the Hollywood press reporting that Robert Stigwood (producer of *Grease*) was considering casting the pair in the title roles of a film version of *Evita*. Both Olivia and Travolta were keen on the project, 'That is the one role I've always thought would be incredible, but I've given up any hope of getting it,' said Olivia at the time. It appears the whole idea was plagued with problems. Stigwood had wanted Ken Russell to direct, but he had cast Liza Minnelli in the lead role of Eva Peron. Tim Rice (the show's co-author) was insistent that Elaine Paige, who first brought the role to life on the West End stage, should play the part of Eva. Russell walked out, leaving the film with no director and no stars, a position that had Paige commenting: 'If they don't hurry up and do it, I'll be too old to play the part!'[1]

At about the same time, a press release was issued stating that Olivia was heading for Broadway to play Marilyn Monroe in a new stage show to be called *Marilyn – An American Fable*. The £1.5 million production was later to have been made into a film. 'It's a very exciting prospect,' said Olivia. 'Playing this part would be a welcome change from the goody-goody image people keep saying I have.

---

[1]The movie version of *Evita* would eventually be made fourteen years later starring Madonna in the lead and directed by Alan Parker.

I've always wanted to do something like this.' Needless to say this project never got off the ground either. It would later be announced that Olivia and John Travolta had signed with Twentieth Century Fox to appear in a romantic comedy to be called *Second Chance*, due to commence filming in June.

But the year was to take a turn for the worse, when on February 4th, it was announced to the world that Karen Carpenter had died after a seven-year battle with anorexia nervosa. Karen and Livvy had been close friends for almost a decade, sharing holidays and secrets; their friendship had been a crutch for Karen to lean on during the darkest moments of her illness. The two women had met at Karen's New York hotel only days before her death, when Olivia had commented on how well Karen was looking, and the two had discussed plans for a long weekend together in San Diego as soon as they both were back on the West Coast. 'There was a kind of loneliness to her voice,' Olivia said to Ray Coleman in his biography of *The Carpenters*. 'There's a warmth there, but also a kind of longing. The world has lost a heaven-sent voice.'

Filming began in Hollywood in June for the new Twentieth Century Fox romantic comedy *Second Chance*, starring Travolta and Olivia along with cinema stalwarts Oliver Reed, Charles Durning, Beatrice Straight and Scatman Crothers. The storyline revolves around two main actors who, as star-matched lovers, are given one week to fall in love and save the world! Travolta was cast as Zach Melon – a want-to-be inventor, whose luck expires when his zany inventions (including a 'barking' doorbell and edible sunglasses) fail to sell and loan sharks decide to call in their debts. Olivia plays Debbie Wylder – an aspiring actress, working as a bank teller, who becomes involved with Zach following a disastrous bank robbery attempt at her window. 'The film is a love story about two people who need to be redeemed,' said John Hertzfeld, who was making his debut as a director on the picture. 'I think everyone would like the opportunity of doing things differently, and this is the story of two people who get the chance.'

Travolta was drawn to the script by its affectionate resolve: 'Love builds and gets stronger in the film. Even though people are complex and may lapse in their moral behaviour, love can win out in the end – if they remain true to one another.' Olivia felt the timing was perfect, as a performer she was growing more confident and was eager to put her experience of two years ago well behind her.

'When I read the script,' she explained, 'I loved the character. She was strong and also just a little obnoxious, which I thought would be a good stretch for me.' The film was to be a first for Olivia for two reasons: it would be her first non-singing role and the first time (and only time to date) her fans would hear her use a four-letter word on film! But working with Travolta again was the main reason for accepting: 'It's marvellous to work together again, there's a special kind of chemistry between us.'

The finished product was released with the new title *Two of a Kind* on December 12th in the United States, where one critic wrote of the £16 million movie: 'The worst movie of the year!' It would be another two months before it reached British cinemas, when it was greeted with the same amount of venom: 'They should have burned the whole film,' one said. 'There's not one comment, one line of idiotic dialogue that makes the slightest iota of sense.' He went on to call Travolta 'plain stupid' and Olivia – 'a tone deaf, hopeless Australian mannequin'. Despite the critics choice words and flagging ticket sales at worldwide cinemas, the picture eventually grossed $25 million in the USA alone, with the film's soundtrack album, which featured four new tracks by Olivia, faired well on Bill-

board's Hot 100 gaining platinum sales. The title track –
'Twist of Fate' which went into the top ten for her in the
singles charts, was a new direction musically, featuring
Canadian-born David Foster as producer. Replacing long-
time associate John Farrar at the helm, Foster, who had
been actively involved with rock group Chicago in the
Seventies, had been keen to work with Olivia for some
time: 'I've always loved Olivia's singing,' he said.

To accompany the soundtrack, Olivia filmed yet another music video for her four songs, visiting England to
film three of the four. Arlene Philips, who had been a
successful dancer in the Seventies with dance troop Hot
Gossip, was brought in to choreograph and Travolta flew
in specially for two of the videos. A fourth track, 'Shaking
You', was filmed in Venice.

Wedding Bells Ring...

As 1984 got under way, so did Olivia's career, with another top forty hit in the USA with 'Living in Desperate Times' (again from the film's soundtrack). Olivia was later invited to record a duet with Barry Gibb on his forthcoming album, *Now Voyager*, but it was following a get-together with John and Pat Farrar that Olivia's career would change direction. 'I commented on how I was feeling homesick for Australia and meat pies,' said Olivia. The following morning, having slept on the idea, Pat called Olivia with the suggestion of opening up an Aussie-style milk bar, serving malt shakes, vegemite sandwiches and Australian magazines. The seed was planted and in the summer of that year the first Koala Blue bar opened on Melrose Avenue in Hollywood.

Nobody could have envisaged the success their joint enterprise would achieve; within a year of opening they would have a second outlet in the Los Angeles area, followed by others in San Diego and interstate. Having started out as milk bar, they eventually expanded to incorporate Australian fashions – featuring such designers as Stuart Membry, Ken Done and Briony Gyngelle – and having their own fashion line twice a year. Other outlets were opened worldwide, including Tokyo, Sydney and Melbourne, Olivia's named involvement guaranteed the venture a success. This was finally rewarded in 1989, when Olivia was named 'Celebrity Businesswoman of the Year' by the American Association of Retail Merchandisers.

'It's wonderful!' said Pat Farrar to Australia's *New Idea* magazine in 1984. 'All the Aussie tours come to the store, we have become a main stop before Disneyland. Australians living in the US rely on us for their papers and magazines from home.' Pat was to take on a more active role in the running of Koala Blue, working full-time in the shop, compared with Olivia, who 'can't be involved on a daily basis because of her career'.

Having been a quiet year on the music career front, December proved to be an important month in Olivia's calendar. After years of being questioned as to when she planned to marry and even more years striving to find the right man – Matt Lattanzi being only Olivia's third 'serious' relationship – Olivia finally went and tied the knot on December 15th at her Malibu home. A reported story had Olivia 'secretly buying her own wedding ring'. Apparently, Olivia picked out and paid for the ring, later sending her secretary to the jewellers to collect the A\$35,000 diamond clustered gem and delivering it to the groom on the day of the ceremony.

Not having ventured into a recording studio for over two years (her previous album *Physical* had been in 1981, but a guest appearance on the *Two of a Kind* soundtrack was in 1983), Olivia finally decided to make a return to pop music with a collection to be produced by long-time friend John Farrar. The album, seductively titled *Soul Kiss* ('It's about kissing feet!' Olivia would later quip in a promotional interview) would prove to be her most controversial to date. With the title track and others: 'Overnight Observation' and 'You Were Great, How Was I?', many questioned where the usually 'coy', 'squeaky clean' Olivia was heading! Then the album cover went one step further, featuring pictures taken by family friend Helmut Newton (who had helped Rona's modelling career get started in the late Sixties). The front showed Olivia in a tight-fitting, off-the-shoulder dress, seductively caressing a leather sofa; but it was the back cover that shocked the majority of her record buying public. Olivia was wearing only a skin-tight pair of riding jodhpurs, a strategically placed scarf and wielding a crop facing a mirror – was this Olivia's attempt at soft porn? 'Helmut Newton has a way of encouraging you to do things you wouldn't normally do,' said Olivia at the time. 'Although the scarf is definitely taped into position. It is only my back I'm showing off!' Olivia would later admit, during an interview for British television in 1995: 'I was never really happy with that picture. I don't know why we took it now.'

Both single and album were issued in September, with MCA Records in the States and with a new deal on Phonogram's Mercury label in Europe. Olivia had ended a twelve-year association with EMI Records in 1983, following reports that she was dissatisfied with their lack of sales promotion on her releases. The first single, 'Soul Kiss', received regular airplay on American radio, achieving a respectable top twenty placing on both Billboard's Hot 100 and the Adult Contemporary Chart, although in Britain it failed to catch on despite an attractive twelve-inch remix version that seemed to be selling well. The album went gold in the US but only managed three weeks in the UK charts.

Little did Olivia know at the time of recording, but she was actually pregnant with her first child. A planned long-form video of the ten tracks, as had previously proved a success in 1981 with 'Physical', was cut short after just five, when Olivia found filming a strain six months into her pregnancy. The videos were released accompanied by a promotional interview, with Olivia introducing each track.

It's a Girl…

On American television in December 1985, both Olivia and Matt spoke of their impending parenthood: 'Olivia was born to be a mother' said Matt. 'It's probably the most important thing that's ever happened to me,' said Olivia. On February 16th, 1986, Olivia gave birth to a 5lb 6oz baby girl, with Matt at her side. The parents decided on the names Chloe-Rose. 'Before I had Chloe,' Olivia went on to say, 'I used to think – What if I don't love my baby as much as I love my dog? I know it sounds stupid, but when you love your animals that much you can't imagine it – but when she was born, my dog became a dog!'

Even though she had cancelled the majority of her work schedule, Olivia did honour a recording session with long-time friend and producer David Foster, who had invited her to guest on a duet for his forthcoming solo album. The duet, 'The Best of Me', had been composed by Foster, along with Jeremy Lubbock (another familiar name throughout Olivia's music career) and Richard Marx. 'When we recorded the vocals for this,' recalls Foster, 'Olivia had just had her baby. So we had to go over to her house with a special recording truck.' The track was issued on single in early May, but failed to gain any momentum in either the British or American charts, although in Foster's native Canada it went to number thirty-two. Ironically, in 1990, Cliff Richard would choose to record a cover version of the song and issue it as his one hundredth UK single release – taking it into the top five!

Olivia took to motherhood like a duck to water, cancelling all her work commitments to take care of the baby, and making only the occasional appearance to visit her Los Angeles-based boutique – Koala Blue. 'I wanted Chloe to have a mother and not be raised by nannies,' she said. 'I even held play groups at the house.' Both Matt and Olivia were so overjoyed at becoming parents that they decided to try for a second child as soon as possible. With a fortieth birthday fast approaching, Olivia was realistic – 'I realise now that I don't have a lot of time left to become a mother again.'

The family spent Christmas 1987 in California, but flew out to Australia for New Year to be with Olivia's family. January 1st, 1988, was to start the beginning of Australia's bicentennial celebrations with a live television broadcast, featuring a guest appearance by Olivia performing a live acoustic version of a self-penned tribute – 'It's Always Australia for Me'. This was followed by an appearance at Sydney's Entertainment Centre on January 26th in front of the Prince and Princess of Wales, where the song was given another warm reception. Olivia also performed a duet with old friend Cliff Richard.

Work also began on her fourteenth studio album, as Olivia decided the timing was right to try for a comeback after a three-year absence from recording. Although her work schedule had been low, Olivia had used her time creatively, appearing as co-composer on several of the new songs for the album. The title track, 'The Rumour', had been composed by Elton John and Bernie Taupin following a call from Olivia: 'I needed one more song and I asked Elton if he would write one for me. He was going away on holiday for a few days and when he got back he had written the lyrics. He's amazing!' He also offered to produce the song as well as providing backing vocals.

But the recording sessions were marred by the reappearance of a certain 'fan' who had been plaguing Olivia with letters and phone calls for almost a year. On one occasion, claiming he was a songwriter, he gained admission to the grounds of Olivia's Malibu home. Matt arrived home to find both his wife and child in a state of panic and distress. Within a year, Olivia, along with fellow performers Cher and Sheena Easton, would again find herself the object of another 'profile' – a description given by California State Police to individuals who are listed as 'a danger to public personalities' – who had terrorised the three stars in 1984 claiming that Olivia was 'an evil impostor' who was 'out to destroy him'. During a BBC radio interview in 1992, Olivia spoke of the experiences: 'I try not to dwell on the thought of it too much, because I think that can sometimes create the fear.'

Once The Rumour Spreads...

With the finishing touches made on the album, which was to be a more adult-orientated set of tracks compared with previous albums – covering such diverse topics as Aids, the environment and single parenthood, it was released in September in the USA and Europe, to good reviews. Bob Hoerburger, of the *American Music Press*, wrote: 'It's a bit of a jolt to hear Olivia Newton-John singing about Aids and the environment. For eighteen years she has been one of pop music's prettiest faces; now she just wants a little respect, and with *The Rumour* she earns it.' Whereas Keith Sharp of Britain's *New Musical Express* said: 'There's a new sense of maturity here. The lyrical message of songs like "It's Not Heaven" and "Get Out" are spiced with a sense of reality only a mature person can envision.' He did go on to say that one fault on the album was the tendency to over-production, saying that Olivia's 'plaintive vocal style works best when kept simple and not forced to battle against overblown arrangements.' The album fared better in the Australian charts compared with the American and British – attaining only a low placing in both.

Instead of the usual foray into long-form video media for the album, Olivia cashed in on the two hundredth anniversary celebrations in Australia, filming a one hour special entitled *Olivia – Down Under*, which featured her travelling around the vast continent, performing songs from the album. *Australian TV Weekly* wrote, 'The show's perhaps the best tourism commercial this country could ever hope to find!'

Olivia ended the year on a happy note, when she discovered she was carrying her second child. However, the joy was short-lived: Olivia miscarried mid-term. Speaking to the *Los Angeles Times*, she said: 'I was over the moon when I became pregnant in the summer. I wanted Chloe to have a brother or sister. But I haven't given up hope. I will be trying again as quickly as possible.' Talking on the same occasion was fellow performer and close friend Bette Midler: 'We share each other's joy and we share each other's pain', having recently had a miscarriage herself.

As the new year got under way, Olivia continued to concentrate on being a mother and businesswoman – her partnership in Koala Blue proving highly lucrative. She was invited to take part in a charity recording to help raise awareness of the mass destruction of the world's rainforests. The single, 'Spirit of the Forest', was to feature other guest vocalists – Kate Bush, Belinda Carlisle, Mick Fleetwood, Bonnie Rait and The Ramones, to name a few – and would be issued by the Virgin record label. Following Olivia's involvement, she was approached by the United Nations: 'I just mentioned that if there was ever anything I could do… and they said – well, as a matter of fact, how would you like to be our National Ambassador to the Environment?'

With Olivia's public image and obvious dedication to the environment, accepting the post became all the more important to her. Especially having been a founding board member of the 'Earth Communication Office' the previous year, her name helped to put across the cause: 'I don't care if people are cynical as long as I get their attention; and even if they think I'm a jerk, I don't particularly care,' she commented at the time. 'Pollution doesn't stop at borders; we are an endangered species. We need clean air, clean

101

water and clean food to survive.'

This was brought all the more to the fore later in the year, when after an eighteen-year association with MCA Records, Olivia opted out of re-signing with them following a dispute over a conflict of ideas for her next recording venture. After the commercial failure of *The Rumour* the previous year, MCA wanted her to follow up with another set of contemporary songs; but since the birth of Chloe in 1986, Olivia had wanted to record an album of lullabies.

She approached Geffen Records, and after a meeting with their A&R man, John Kalodner, she was amazed when his response was a positive one. Recording took place in Australia, accompanied by the Melbourne Philharmonic Orchestra. Olivia's renditions of the standards: 'The Way You Look Tonight', 'The Twelfth of Never', 'You'll Never Walk Alone' and 'Reach Out for Me' gained a mixed reception.

'The combinations of Newton-John's often ethereal-sounding voice and super-sweetie-pie songs could have easily made this album into the equivalent of a hypoglycemia attack,' wrote Ralph Novak of *Rolling Stone*. 'But she tempers the material with just enough restraint and makes it into one long lullaby, as soothing as the songs suggest.'

Warm And Tender was issued in November, featuring a dust cover printed on recycled paper – Olivia's personal attempt at introducing the recording industry to the fates of the planet's fast diminishing rainforests – and an inner sleeve providing Olivia with the perfect opportunity to promote her new-found position as Goodwill Ambassador to the United Nations. Ten important tips on how to save the environment were given, along with a closing message from the singer:

'Time is running out, but it's not too late. Let's teach

ourselves and our children to value all forms of life. Let's go forward positively with love. We can and we must turn things around.'

PART FOUR

It would be un-American not to love Olivia Newton-John.

Doug Sheehan (co-star in *A Mom for Christmas*)

Christmas Magic...

As 1990 got underway, Olivia's involvement with the United Nations as Goodwill Ambassador to the Environment began to take hold when, along with John Denver, she co-hosted the *Earth Day Special* – which was telecast live from Brazil to over one hundred and thirty countries worldwide.

She was also approached by NBC television about the prospect of doing her own television series. 'I met with people from NBC and we talked about what I would like to do,' she explained to Jerry Buck of *USA Magazine*. 'A month later this script arrived. Production was starting in Cincinnati in two weeks and I had to make up my mind in a hurry.'

Based on the book, *A Mom by Magic* by Barbara Dillon, it gave Olivia the chance to work with fellow Australian George Miller (who had directed *The Man from Snowy River*). 'The film appealed to me,' says Olivia, 'because it was about Christmas and being a mom.' Although the prospect of going in front of the cameras again was a little daunting, having had a seven-year break from acting: 'It's like anything – riding a bike or riding a horse – if you haven't done something for a long time, then it takes a lot of confidence to get out there and do it again,' she says. 'I hope that I've matured some in that time,' she continues. 'The character I play has a bit of fantasy about her, but she is also a mom which reflects an aspect of my life I feel comfortable with.'

The storyline centres around twelve-year-old Jessica, who lives alone with her widowed father whose passion for work exceeds his love for his daughter. Whilst shopping one day, Jessica notices a family of shop mannequins and wistfully wishes she had 'a mom like that'. At the stroke of midnight on Christmas Eve, there is a knock at their door and Jessica's wish has been granted, when Amy [Olivia] walks in. What followed was nothing more than Disney-esque family entertainment, with love blossoming and hearts breaking and love reunited again. Veteran actress Doris Roberts, who plays Wilomena – the sales assistant who helps young Jessica's dream come true – says of the story: 'It's based on love, nourishment, wonderful humour and magic and caring. It's a wonderful story!'

Olivia's casting as the store mannequin who comes to life appealed to her because she gets the chance to play comedy, with one or two off-the-cuff one-liners. 'Amy gets her first chance at life outside the store, but everything she knows is from out of books,' explains Olivia. 'She's been brought to life and she's human. The only things she doesn't know about are behaviour and feelings.'

Also, working with twelve-year-old Juliet Scorcey was a joy. The young actress instantly befriended five-year-old Chloe, who on most days accompanied Olivia, and that made for an all-round family atmosphere. 'Maybe if I hadn't had a daughter of my own I wouldn't have had that rapport with Juliet,' says Olivia of her young co-star. 'She kind of treated me like her other daughter on set,' said Juliet of her screen Mom. 'She would often say – There's my two girls. She's fun.'

The film's director, George Miller, praised his star highly: 'She's always had a vivacious quality. Now that she is a mom herself – I think that has had a profound effect on her personality and that comes through in her acting. She has a depth that just makes her magnificent.' On one occasion, when Olivia was involved in an emotionally charged scene that required her to cry – an emotion that the most accomplished of actresses find difficult to achieve – she delivered on cue. 'I was speechless,' exclaims Miller. 'She did it in one take.'

The film, which was made especially for television, aired on the NBC Network in America on December 17th, 1990, attaining a top ten position in the ratings for that week.

In November, following the successful West End opening of the new stage version of *Grease*, Polygram International (who own the rights to the original motion picture soundtrack) decided to issue a special *Grease Megamix* single featuring 'You're the One That I Want', 'Greased Lightning' and 'Summer Nights'. It took off in British nightclubs in a big way, going straight into the singles chart at number fourteen on December 9th and eventually peaking at number three in the new year. A subsequent follow-up – *The Grease Dream Mix*, featuring extracts from 'Grease', 'Sandy' and 'Hopelessly Devoted to You' – failed to have the same impact, falling short of the top forty at number forty-seven. The soundtrack was also given a rebirth, entering the top ten again, proving once more that fourteen years down the line *Grease* is still the word!

Double Whammy...

In a career that had spanned two decades and had crossed many boundaries, it seemed hard to comprehend that by the beginning of 1992 the bubble could start to burst. Her joint clothing empire, Koala Blue, had hit financial problems in the midst of a worldwide recession, with many franchises suing Olivia and Pat Farrar claiming that the company's problems were largely due to mismanagement on their part. A report in the *Wall Street Journal* wrote that 'some licensees abused her [Olivia's] celebrity status by dragging their feet when paying for merchandise'. 'They saw me as a wealthy star, so they figured – why pay on time?' said Olivia in the same report. The situation left Pat and Olivia personally liable for over several million dollars worth of Koala Blue debts. 'Both Pat and myself lost a lot more than anyone else,' said Olivia. She would later prefer not to discuss the situation, stating: 'We will be fine. It's a chapter that's closed now, but we got into some business difficulty with a partner and basically we just fell apart, but it was enjoyable whilst it lasted.'

With Olivia's singing career having taken a back seat over the previous nine years – she had only released three studio albums since *Physical* in 1981 – she now felt the time was right to try and tackle a comeback; and with 1992 marking the twenty-first anniversary of her debut single 'If Not For You', what better way than to issue a collection of her greatest hits? *Back to Basics: The Essential Collection*

1971–1992 was put together by Olivia and would also feature four new tracks, all of which had been produced by different people: 'Not Gonna Be the One' (John Farrar), 'Deeper Than a River' (Guy Roche and Diane Warren), a song that Olivia points out 'had been promised to another performer – I had to beg, steal and borrow to record it'; 'I Want to Be Wanted' (Peter Asher) and 'I Need Love' by Giorgio Moroder. The latter song taking her vocal style one step further – 'I never thought I would ever record a dance record!' Olivia exclaimed on Gloria Hunniford's BBC Radio 2 show in June 1992. Bill Sammeth, Olivia's present agent, and Olivia had planned the big comeback, with worldwide public appearances and a stateside concert tour of America, possibly going international if things went well in the States.

She flew to Monaco in early June to co-host the annual World Music Awards with Cliff Richard, an ideal opportunity to promote the new single 'I Need Love', and then on to Britain for interviews, where a special interview was being planned with Terry Wogan on his popular BBC chat show. Her visit was cut short when news reached her that her father was ill – he had been battling cancer of the liver for the last few years. Having spent time with her father in New South Wales, Olivia flew home to Malibu to take a short break before commencing rehearsals for the upcoming concert tour.

Following a routine visit to her own doctor for a checkup, Olivia and the family set off for a weekend away in Seattle. Not long after their arrival, Matt received two phone calls: one was from Olivia's doctor requesting that she visit him as soon as she returned, and the second informed him that Olivia's father had died. July 3rd had always been a day of celebration in the past, it was the birthday of Olivia's older brother Hugh, but this year it was full of heartache. Matt told Olivia of her father's passing away and gave her the chance to mourn before informing her of the second message.

'I had a feeling that something was wrong,' says Olivia. 'Although the mammogram showed nothing – I just knew. Then a biopsy showed a malignant lump in my breast.' Rather than go into hiding and allow the world's press to speculate over her condition, Olivia decided to go public: 'I'm making this information public myself to save inquiring minds ninety-five cents.'

'I'm glad now that I went public. I think it was freeing for me, because I've been holding things like that in,' she explained to John Beverage of Melbourne's *Sun-Herald* newspaper in 1998. 'It's maybe part of the problem in the first place – why we get sick.'

The initial reaction to the news was of fear – fear of not seeing her six-year-old daughter Chloe grow up, fear of not fulfilling her desire to be a parent once more. But many of her closest friends were amazed, if not shocked, at her sense of humour: 'Some people found it very strange, but I remember when I was first diagnosed, I used to ring my friends and make jokes, because they were so freaked out and that was the only way of breaking the ice.'

The news that Olivia Newton-John had breast cancer hit the world's headlines on every front page. 'The wholesome, clean-living, girl-next-door image she had purveyed over the years had sold her short,' as many articles wrote; 'having pioneered the fitness craze with *Physical* long before Jane Fonda jumped on the band-wagon.'

Prior to surgery, Olivia considered every option – eventually deciding to mix Western medicine with Eastern; using meditation and visualisation and positive thinking as guides from a team of healers that included renowned names such as Louise Hay and Deepak Chopra.

She was admitted to Hollywood's Cedar Sinai Hospital

for treatment. 'It's called a modified radical, so they take a lot, but not everything. So I was able to have an implant right away, which was very fortunate,' Olivia later explained in an exclusive interview on American television. 'They do it during surgery so they do it all at the same time. You lose one and gain a new one. It's like a new friend.' The operation was then followed by six months of chemotherapy. 'Cancer – say the word – we've got to get used to this word,' she continued. 'It always freaks everybody out; but it's just a word that describes a condition and it's not necessarily a fatal condition.'

The worldwide support that followed overwhelmed even Olivia, as thousands upon thousands of letters and cards arrived wishing her well. 'The concern and support from total strangers has been overwhelming,' she says. 'Some had breast cancer and wanted to share their thoughts. Others simply wanted to reach out. Their compassion meant more to me than I can ever say.' As a personal response, Olivia thanked all her well-wishers via a letter printed in *Hello/Hola* magazine.

Olivia's decision to go public was an incentive for other women to take their bodies seriously and listen to them. 'That day in July was the end of a lot of things for me, but I feel very happy to have discovered the cancer early. I tried to be grown up about it, but I was terrified of dying.'

'I went through hell and back, but I'm finally through the worst,' were the headlines in early 1993. 'I've got the cancer licked and I'm going home. After months of going through the worst pain you could imagine – I honestly believe I'm over it, and that's the main decision. It's the decision I've had to make.'

One of the hardest decisions to make was not to tell her daughter Chloe of her illness: 'She had just lost her best friend, Colette, to cancer,' Olivia explained to Beth Kleid on *USA Today*. 'I knew that if I told her, she would think I was going to die.' Then, after it was all over, Chloe heard it from another source, a fellow schoolmate. 'She came running home and said, "Is it true?" I told her it was and promised from then on that I would always tell her everything.'

In the wake of the international news of Olivia's breast cancer ordeal, sales of her *Back to Basics* collection flourished: it went to number twelve in the British charts and number two in Australia. All career comeback plans had been aborted due to her surgery treatment and recuperation; and Olivia returned to her avocado farm in Byron Bay, surrounded by the Mt Warning Range of mountains in the east and the McPherson Range in the west – what could be more peaceful?

Olivia's recovery period turned out to be a creative one. She planned to write a book about her experience with cancer, but went on to co-write a children's book. *A Pig Tale*, which started out as a joke between Olivia and friend Brian Hurst: 'I was making up silly jokes, like, "Oh! What a pig!"; and I thought it might be a good idea to turn it around and have a pig joking, "What a human!" Brian thought it was a good idea for a story, so we started working on it.'

It turned out to be a story for children told in rhyme about a homely family of pigs who collect junk and put it to good use – three issues very close to Olivia's heart: the environment, children and animals. 'I wanted it to have an environmental theme, but we had to be very careful not to make it too heavy. I sent the last verse off to Simon & Schuster and waited with bated breath. They loved it and even agreed to print it on recycled paper, their first children's book they'd done that way.' As Goodwill Ambassador for the United Nations Environmental Program she said: 'It would have felt wrong putting out a book on glossy paper!' As an added bonus, profits from the

114

book's sales were to go to the Colette Chuda Environmental Fund, which had been set up two years earlier in memory of nine-year-old Colette, the daughter of Olivia's best friend Nancy Gould Chuda, who had died of cancer, to help fund research into the links between the environment and cancer.

All Over the World...

In Australia, Olivia was approached by television networks with offers of work, where figures in the region of A$50,000 were being quoted by national press. She picked up on only two of the options: her very own wildlife series – *Human/Nature with Olivia Newton-John* and a three-episode guest appearance in the Australian soap *Banjo Patterson's 'The McGregor Saga'*. The former gave Olivia the chance to explore the relationships between humans and the environment, on several occasions forcing her to face her phobias, which included snakes and flying. 'I did all the things I swore I would never do,' she explained to *Australian Woman's Weekly* in June 1994. 'I went up in a crane, fifty metres into the roof of a rainforest in Panama. I am terrified of heights and I had to fight off that feeling of wanting to jump out and fly.' The first series took her all over South America – including visits to Belize, Costa Rica, Yucatan in Central Mexico and to Texas, where she spent time with actor Patrick Swayze at his stud farm.

'We've had some nightmare trips,' enthused the show's producer Scott Young. 'We've had guns pointed our way in Central America, toxic hotel rooms in Russia and death drives in Greece, but Olivia was a dream.' He was full of admiration for his presenter, saying: 'I've worked with a lot of people of her calibre and they can be pretentious, but Olivia will try anything. She never wanted to work with snakes, we got her one day with a snake around her head and then her waist, and she was making jokes.' As well as facing her phobias, Olivia was also enticed into marine diving off the coast of Lizard Island (near the coast of far northern Queensland, Australia), tentatively warning Young: 'Scott, remember I'm a mother and if anything happens to me I'll kill you.'

In between the heat and humidity of filming in Central America, Olivia also found the time to honour her second deal with Australian television – a guest appearance in the soap *The McGregor Saga* for Channel Seven. In the three-episode appearance, she played the part of an American searching for her long lost father in the Victorian gold fields in nineteenth-century Australia. It was to be Olivia's first attempt at television acting, and speaking to *Woman's Day* magazine she explained that she felt a little uneasy at first. Her co-stars included well-known personalities Andrew Clarke, Wendy Hughes, Victoria Tennant and Guy Pearce. 'The first day I walked out on set, I looked around and everybody knew each other except me. I hadn't acted in years. But when you've had to face a few major things, as I have had to over the past couple of years, then little challenges like starting a new job don't really matter.'

Many were surprised at Olivia's keenness to get back to work so soon after her brush with cancer, but the offers had been appealing to her. 'I wanted another excuse to be in Australia, and for once it seemed I was getting to play an adult role,' she said. 'I've played so many little girl roles, this was woman's stuff.'

I Still Call Australia Home...

In September of 1994, Olivia surprised everybody by announcing that she was finally going to become an 'ocker Aussie citizen'. Despite her British birth, she had, for the majority of her career, been widely regarded as an Australian and she said, 'here is where my real roots are'.

'My mother and father became Australians when they moved here in the Fifties, but I've always travelled on a British passport – it was easier in the early days,' she said to *Woman's Day* magazine. 'Now it's important for me to be an Aussie.'

Although she had spent only her early teenage years in Melbourne, before flying back to England to start her career, and the occasional long holiday with her family – Olivia had always regarded Australia as her home. Following her recuperation after her cancer, she felt that the time was right to make it more permanent. 'It feels right to be living in Australia right now,' she said. 'We are happy here – it's a wonderful place to live and to raise a child.' Eight-year-old Chloe being a driving force behind her decision to take the plunge: 'She is so excited, she's wanted to be an Aussie so badly. She loves living here and going to school. This is her home now.'

Olivia was ecstatic after taking the oath of allegiance and receiving her record of citizenship: 'I'm so happy at finally becoming an Australian. I just haven't been living here long enough in the past to be able to.'

Mother Earth Calling...

Her recovery period also proved creative on a musical front – with the birth of a new studio album of songs written by Olivia herself. *Gaia: One Woman's Journey* was borne out of her experiences with breast cancer and chemotherapy: 'Not Gonna Give into It'; the demise of Koala Blue – 'No Matter What You Do'; and her ever-growing concern for the environment – 'Don't Cut Me Down'. 'It became a catharsis for all my emotions,' she told Gloria Hunniford on BBC Radio 2. 'I would wake up in the early hours of the morning with these songs in my head, and have to go into another room to write them down without disturbing the rest of the house.'

'These songs were all written in a short space of time between starting my chemotherapy through to the end,' explained Olivia to Marjory Bennett of Melbourne's *Sun-Herald* newspaper. 'I needed, through my music, to reach people about the state of our planet. It's something I am very concerned about.' She added that there are also 'positive songs about not giving into pain and being strong.' One song in particular that Olivia is eager to point out refers to her first reaction to the news that she had breast cancer: 'Many people automatically respond with "Why me?", but I felt "Why me? Why not me?"' The track – 'Why Me', doesn't question her condition, but tries to reinforce the conditions of living: it exhorts us to live for the moment, taking time to smell the roses, and to take whatever life throws at us on the chin – encouraging words from a woman who has faced so many personal dilemmas in such a short period of time.

Co-producer of the album, Murray Burns, was very supportive of the project: 'She's a gifted, natural songwriter who never had the confidence, till now, to get down and do it. It's very much a woman speaking from the heart.'

Olivia's decision to put her own money into the album was out of pure emotional desire to get the songs on tape, knowing that by approaching a record company with the idea would only be met with the usual scepticism and the question: 'Where is the hit single?' 'I wanted to make this album whether it was a success or not!' And a success it turned out to be – on its release in Australia (with Festival Records, who Olivia has been with from the very beginning) it entered their album charts at number seven, attaining gold sales status within three weeks. Due to her lack of representation outside of Australasia, it would be almost a year before the album would be issued anywhere else in the world, with independent label D# Sharp taking the initiative in Britain. Although despite an intensive three week promotional trip by Olivia, the album only spent four weeks in the charts, reaching number thirty-three.

Whilst still in Australia, Olivia made her first public appearances on television since her treatment – if only to put to rest press speculation that she was selling her Malibu home and returning to New South Wales in order to live out her remaining few months! Admittedly, her home had been put on the market (at a reported US$8 million), but simply because Olivia and Matt had built a new eco-friendly beach house on the coast: 'I had owned this piece of land for about twelve years, and for ten of those we had discussed building a house on it,' said Olivia.

The house was built primarily of plaster, wood and stone, with the materials used being environmentally friendly. 'We used non-toxic paints and all the wood stains were non-poisonous,' continues Olivia. 'And, most importantly, all the wood we used was taken from forests that are harvested sustainably – they only take one tree out of the forest instead of cutting them all down.'

Back in Australia, she made a rare live appearance in Brisbane, Queensland, singing one song from the new album – *No Other Love* – at the concert for the spina bifida charity Challenge at the city's entertainment centre. Olivia confessed to more than a slight attack of nerves before the event, but coped calmly with the strain of an afternoon's tight rehearsal schedule – with all performers being pushed to their limits by a relentless deadline. Her appearance on the stage confirmed the loyalty of her fans and Olivia was visibly affected by the reception they gave her.

With the bulk of her promotional work for the album finished, it was straight back to the United States to finalise a deal with CBS television network to appear in what was to be her second TV film – another seasonal, family show titled *A Christmas Romance*, co-starring Gregory Harrison and Olivia's daughter, Chloe, making her acting debut.

In the production, which was filmed in the snows of British Columbia in Canada, Olivia's widowed character and two children find themselves snowed in at their cabin with obstinate bank manager-come-scrooge Harrison, who has been sent to evict them. 'It's a kind of don't-judge-a-book-by-its-cover-type story,' says Olivia. It comes as no surprise that the two main characters eventually warm to each other, and love blossoms over the festive season. 'I can relate to her loneliness and to the pain she's going through,' concludes Olivia, referring to her experiences over the previous two years; but what truly attracted her to the script was the fact that – 'there's no sex. It's a family movie. My child can watch it. My child is in it…'

'I was so proud of her. It was wonderful to see her

blossom as an actress,' said Olivia of working with her third-grader daughter Chloe Lattanzi. 'But it was also difficult because I had to divide myself from being the mother and being the actress.'

The film aired on the CBS network on the run-up to Christmas 1994 and went on to a achieve top ten rating – proving once again that Olivia's absence from the music charts certainly hasn't dented her popularity with her American fans!

And I'll Cry if I Want To...

It seemed that following her brush with cancer Olivia's career was on a roll, having ventured into more television and film work than at any other point in her twenty-year career. And 1995 showed no signs of her slowing up – with two new projects in the offing. The first project was a second teaming with *Grease* director Randal Kleiser in a low budget drama about how Aids affects the lives of a close-knit group of friends. The second project was a new recording venture with long-time friend Cliff Richard on the album version of his forthcoming stage production *Heathcliff*.

Kleiser wrote *It's My Party* over a two year period and filmed it in only twenty-five days. The story revolves around Nick Stark (played by Eric Roberts) a Los Angeles-based architect graced with vitality, good looks, loyal friends, a thriving career, down-to-earth attitude and an irreverent sense of humour. Although he looks healthy, he has been fighting off Aids-related illnesses for some time; and now, just before Christmas, he discovers that untreatable brain lesions (progressive multifocal leukoencephalpathy) will break down all his faculties within days. Nick has decided long ago that he won't linger, but will die with dignity – he intends to savour his remaining time by gathering everyone he loves for a two-day farewell party. Through flashbacks, Nick and Brandon (his former partner) recall good times together, friends they lost to

Aids, and the devastating effect that Nick's illness has had on their relationship.

Once the screenplay was completed, Kleiser, along with producer Joel Thurm, began assembling their cast. Despite working within the constraints of a small budget, the filmmakers were able to gather an impressive group of actors who were passionate about the script. 'Everybody is working in this movie for scale, so we looked for people who would be into what the movie had to say,' said Thurm, who was delighted to find such high-calibre actors as Marlee Matlin, Roddy McDowall, Bruce Davison and Gregory Harrison actually calling him to express their interest.

Olivia was eager to work with her *Grease* director again, but was also motivated by the film's themes. 'The film is about celebrating friends and family,' she says. 'It's about love and caring for people; it's about loss and reunion.' Of her director she was full of praise: 'Randal makes everyone feel calm and comfortable like no other director I've worked with. He has quiet control of the set, and because of that things are tension-free.'

Olivia's character, Linda Bingham, is at the centre of one of the story's sub-plots – her marriage is breaking up and her teenage son Andrew, played by Devon Gummersall, is in the process of 'coming out', a situation that puts him at odds with his father. 'It was challenging for me in that it was probably the first serious thing I've done,' explains Olivia. 'Because the Christmas tele-films were kind of light – so for me that was important.'

'I've lost friends to Aids. I've been in the room when my friend's brother died, so it struck a chord with me. And after my own experiences (with cancer) I could relate to the humour in it.'

United Artists Pictures released the film mid-year, to rave reviews across America: '*It's My Party* is right on target, you can't help but love this movie,' wrote Bob Healy of *Satellite Network News*. 'It's the party of the season,' wrote Stephen Suban in *Details Magazine*. When the film was eventually given its London premiere at the Gay and Lesbian Festival in March 1996, it came in fourth on their list of films for the year, although it never received a nationwide release.

It Had To Be...

For almost two decades Cliff Richard had been talking about writing, producing and starring in a new rock stage version of Emily Brontë's classic love story *Wuthering Heights*, but the timing was never right, and finding the best team of writers proved difficult. Having first met Tim Rice (one half of the successful Andrew Lloyd-Webber/Tim Rice partnership) in the late Sixties, it would be almost a quarter of a century later that they would eventually decide to work together; when, in 1991, to Rice's astonishment, Cliff called to see if he would be interested in contributing to a complete album's worth of material.

Cliff had already approached John Farrar, who agreed to come on board to compose and produce the music. He had also put to Olivia the idea of her recording the vocal part of the show's heroine, Cathy: 'There are plenty of great singers I could have asked,' explains Cliff. 'But I knew Olivia could eat these songs and spit them out. And we look and sound good together.' Olivia jumped at the opportunity of working with Cliff again. And with both John Farrar and Olivia on board – 'how could I refuse?' said Tim Rice.

The plan was to record an album of vocal selections from the original show – five of which would feature guest vocals by Olivia as Cathy, although there was no suggestion of Olivia taking the role when the show went on stage the following year in Birmingham. Vocally the part was a major challenge for Olivia, especially when a promotional clip for the duo's first single release, 'Had To Be', was filmed: 'Cathy is not the nicest of people,' says Olivia. 'Although she loves Heathcliff, she decides to marry someone wealthy and with social standing. Giving up her love for Heathcliff and leaving him in his torment for the rest of his living days.'

'She is strong but full of anger and resentment. Understanding that background gives me an edge in my performance.' Both Cliff and Olivia decided not to discuss characterisation prior to recording or filming their segments to give the tracks a touch of mystery both to each other and the listener.

'Had To Be' was issued on single by EMI Records in November, an, following an appearance on *The Royal Variety Performance* on November 25th, for which Olivia flew into London especially to make a guest appearance, stormed straight into the British singles chart at number twenty-two. Music pundits had the single tipped to be the year's Christmas number one, but over-estimated, when the following week it disappeared from the top forty. The album faired better though, breaking the top twenty at number fifteen and going gold.

Private Lives...

Amid all the publicity and hype that surrounded the album's release, it was hard to see the pain that was hiding behind those famous hazel eyes as Olivia's private life slowly crumbled around her. After ten years of marriage to Matt, they had finally reached a point in their relationship where a separation was imminent. Olivia has constantly guarded her privacy, and no matter what the circumstances has battled through regardless. Press speculation pinpointed the breakdown to the time of the breast cancer ordeal, claiming the pressure of the situation had put a strain on the marriage.

In true Olivia style, the barriers were raised and the family faced their obstacles head on, taking into consideration ten-year-old Chloe and the effect the break-up would have on her. By this time Matt was spending the majority of his time living and working in Australia, presenting a television show in Sydney. So, Olivia's time was divided between the United States and Australia, accepting offers of work that would fit in around Chloe's school schedule and allowing them time to be together as a family. The couple would eventually accept that a reconciliation wasn't going to happen and would decide on a divorce in 1996.

'I don't want to go into my personal life or talk about relationships,' Olivia said defensively. 'That's private. I'm doing very well on my own. Chloe is thriving and life is good. It's a nice place to be in my life.'

Olivia's sister, Rona, who has been a constant friend and companion over the years, was eager to back up her sister: 'I think Olivia's discovered that happiness comes from within. If you can get to a stage where you feel good about yourself, then you don't need anybody else. She knows that money doesn't buy you happiness and neither can anybody else. It has to be you. You can be in love with a great guy and have all the money in the world and still be miserable.'

Personal problems aside, Olivia continued with her career, filming a second series of her successful Australian series *Wildlife* and also entering into discussions with Youngheart Productions (the company behind the successful children's movie *Ferngully: The Last Rainforest*) about the possibility of appearing in a forthcoming $10 million film called *Home for Christmas*, alongside Australian veteran Jack Thompson, to be filmed in their real-life homes in New South Wales.

Jack and Olivia had known each other for some years and had wanted to work together for as long as they cared to remember; also, working with her *Wildlife* producer, Scott Young, on a feature film was enticing to Olivia. 'The idea has been talked about for some months,' she explained to *Woman's Day* magazine. 'It's something I would like to do very much, but it depends on the timing.'

Things couldn't have been better planned, with filming taking place less than a stone's throw from both stars' homes – even the production office was to be based in Byron Bay. The idea was for Olivia to play the part of a mother of two living on a ranch in a typical outback Aussie town, when one day, her son discovers that Santa Claus (Thompson) has crash-landed in their paddock. Being out in the bush Santa has to ditch his traditional red suit and go bush – disguising himself as a swagman until they can patch up his sleigh and get him home in time for Christmas – which turns the whole story into a fish-out-of-water scenario.

It was hoped filming would commence as early as January 1997 ready for a Christmas release, but with other commitments Olivia was unable to agree a schedule and so, for now, the project had to be shelved.

October 13th, 1996, saw Olivia's return to live singing – if only for four numbers. She was invited to host the year's *Lifetime Applauds the Fight Against Breast Cancer* concert – an annual event that for the first time was being recorded for television. Having initiated herself as national spokesperson for breast cancer awareness, it seemed only right that Olivia should be the one to take the lead – introducing fellow artists and public figures who had, at some point in their lives, faced the illness. Her work in the area would officially be recognised two years later when she accepted the Cadillac concept Humanitarian Award for supporting breast cancer work.

Back to Basics...

Over the ensuing two years Olivia took on even more television work. She guested on several American sitcoms and appeared live at charity events, which most recently included the CHEC[1] Symposium in Sundance, Utah and the Operation Smile concert in Nashville. Although a second concert appearance in Nashville, a thirty-minute set at the annual Nashville Fan Fair, was marred by the unpublicised presence of a stalker who had apparently been making death threats over the Internet. This forced Olivia only to make the performance and not allow any publicity interviews afterwards.

Most recently there was a national tour of Australasia as special guest of old friend Cliff Richard, who celebrated his fortieth anniversary in show business with a world tour. It had been sixteen years since Olivia was last on the road, and she was pleased when Cliff suggested she appear as his special guest on the Australian leg of the tour. 'I'm glad to be performing again,' she explained to Melbourne's *Sun-Herald* newspaper. 'But I don't think I'm ready to go it alone just yet. I much prefer the idea of supporting someone else – that way the pressure is less on me.'

The tour included two performances in Auckland and

---

[1]CHEC is the Children's Health and Environmental Coalition – a charity with which Olivia had been actively involved since the death of Colette Chuda in 1991.

Wellington in New Zealand, followed by dates across the breadth of Australia, including two nights at Melbourne Park, Olivia's hometown. Carolyn Alexander, of the *Sun-Herald* newspaper summed up the evening with: '...backed by the Australian Philharmonic Orchestra, Ms Newton-John made a stunning addition to the show.'

'The timing was right to start performing again because I've just recorded my new album – *Back with a Heart* – and it's a gentle way of getting back into it,' she says. 'Singing is wonderful for my soul. That's what I've missed and it's one of the reasons I've come back.'

The timing was certainly right, with 1998 marking the twentieth anniversary of the release of *Grease* – for which Paramount Pictures planned a re-release. What better opportunity to relaunch her career? Olivia spent a lot of time visiting Nashville, appearing at the Operation Smile charity concert, to meet with local writers and composers about the possibility of collaborating on her new songs. 'I wrote a lot of the songs on the new album and some of them reflect what I've been through. The wonderful thing about writing lyrics is the cathartic effect, especially when you're working with other women. You sit there saying: "Oh my God! Have you been there too?" As I've got older, I've become more brave about what I'm willing to put out.'

Having tested the waters in late 1997 featuring on a duet with MCA Nashville's newest signing The Raybon Brothers – 'Falling' – Olivia signed a new, multi-million dollar contract with the label she had left almost a decade earlier over a recording dispute. The contract allowed her creative control over the songs she chose to record and the producers. She chose Nashville as the place to put her twentieth studio album into action. With six different producers at the helm – including John Farrar, Don Cook, Tony Brown and David Foster – it proved an interesting experience.

'Normally, when you work with just one producer, it can take anything up to three months to put the finishing touches to an album,' explains Olivia. 'But with six, it meant I could go from one producer to the next and we'd be finished in less than six weeks.'

Having been away from mainstream music for almost seven years, finding a record company that was willing to take a chance on her was a gamble: 'In this business, if you haven't had a hit for a few years you're considered cold,' she says. 'People of my era are finding it difficult getting record contracts because it's all about youth. I was very focused on what I wanted and luckily I got both the record company and the producers I chose.'

The album hit America's record stores in March to mixed reviews. The *San Diego Tribune* wrote: '*Back with a Heart* finds the singer fitting in easily with the soft pop so many of today's young female singers gravitate towards...' but concluded with, 'The track "Fight for Our Love" – advertised as "her tribute to Fifties-style C&W" – has about as much intensity as a pillow fight!'

Surprisingly, after almost a six year hiatus from the Billboard album charts, *Back with a Heart* debuted at number seventy-one (peaking, to date, at number fifty-nine – although it did fair better on their country charts, at number nine). The first single release, a reworking of her 1974 chart-topper 'I Honestly Love You' (with production credit to David Foster), soared into the charts at number sixty-seven.

When released in Britain by MCA Records in May, the album sailed straight into the country chart's top ten. 'She does reveal a talent for thoughtful, mellow music that avoids being mundane,' wrote Britain's *Country Music International*. 'She does not simply hint at vulnerability; she opens up and pours her heart out!'

As the decade slowly draws to a close, 1998 saw the

twentieth anniversary release of Olivia's most successful film *Grease*, which, when released in the United States in March 1998, received a warm welcome at Graumann's Chinese Theatre in Hollywood. A capacity crowd turned out to see Olivia arrive with fellow cast members Stockard Channing and Jeff Conway. Early ticket returns placed the film at number two for box-office receipts after its first week of release. An intensive worldwide promotional trip followed, bringing her to London for a star-studded premiere at the Empire Cinema, Leicester Square on June 25th followed by an all-star celebrity party in the heart of London's West End, with the proceeds of ticket sales going to the Elton John Aids Foundation. The movie went straight into the week's top five ratings winners – placing it second to the year's other blockbuster, *Titanic*.

As 1998 drew to a close, Olivia showed no signs of slowing up. A successful second concert tour of Australia in a year took place in October and November – Olivia took centre stage with fellow Aussies singer John Farnham and theatre star Antony Warlow in what was billed as 'The Main Event' tour. The year concluded with a sell-out solo mini-tour of North America over the new year, proving that Olivia's career is looking set to last well into the new millennium. She is a star of the twentieth century – one who has outlasted the cynical words of the early Seventies critics, and become one of the most respected female vocalists of her time. Olivia Newton-John is definitely back with a heart.

PART FIVE

I do have high standards, but I don't expect anything from anyone that I don't expect from myself.

Olivia Newton-John

Facts and Figures

1971
Female Vocalist of the Year [*Record Mirror* UK]

1972
Female Vocalist of the Year [*Record Mirror* UK]

1973
Most Promising Female Vocalist [Academy of Country Music USA]
Best Female Vocalist – Country [Grammys USA]

1974
Female Vocalist of the Year [Country Music Association UK]
Female Vocalist of the Year [Country Music Association USA]
Record of the Year – *I Honestly Love You* [Grammys USA]
Best Female Pop Vocal Performance – *I Honestly Love You* [Grammy's USA]
Rising Star Award [AGVA]
Favourite Female Vocalist [People's Choice Awards]
Best Selling Album by a Female – Country – *If You Love Me (Let Me Know)* [National Association of Retail Merchandising]

Best Selling Album by a Female – *If You Love Me (Let Me Know)* [National Association of Retail Merchandising]

Female Artist of the Year [Bobby Poe's Music Awards]

Song of the Year – *I Honestly Love You* [Bobby Poe's Music Awards]

Favourite Female Singer – Pop/Rock [American Music Awards]

Favourite Country Single – *I Honestly Love You* [American Music Awards]

Favourite Female Singer – Country [American Music Awards]

Favourite Country Album – *Let Me Be There* [American Music Awards]

No. 1 Award for Singles and Albums [*Billboard Magazine*]

Top Female Vocalist – Singles [*Record World* USA]

Top Female Vocalist – Albums [*Record World* USA]

No. 1 Female Vocalist – Singles [*Cashbox Magazine* USA]

No. 1 Female Vocalist – Albums [*Cashbox Magazine*]

1975

Female Vocalist of the Year [Country Music Association UK]

Country Music Award – *Please Mr Please* [American Society of Composers, Authors and Publishers (ASCAP)]

Favourite Female Vocalist – Country [American Music Awards]

Favourite Female Vocalist – Rock/Pop [American Music Awards]

Favourite Album – Rock/Pop – *Have You Never Been Mellow* [American Music Awards]

Favourite Female – Country Singles Artist [*Billboard Magazine*]

Favourite Female – Country Albums Artist [*Billboard Magazine*]

Favourite Female – Pop Singles Artist [*Billboard Magazine*]

Favourite Female – Pop Albums Artist [*Billboard Magazine*]
Solo Album of the Year – *Have You Never Been Mellow* [*Record World* USA]
No. 1 Female Vocalist – Singles [*Cashbox Magazine*]
No. 1 Female Vocalist – Albums [*Cashbox Magazine*]

1976

Favourite Female Vocalist [People's Choice Awards]
No. 1 Female Artist [Talent in Action Awards USA]
No. 3 Easy Listening Artist [Talent in Action Awards USA]
No. 3 Pop Singles Artist [Talent in Action Awards USA]
Favourite Female Vocalist – Rock/Pop [American Music Awards]
Top Female Vocalist – Country [*Record World* USA]

1978

Best Selling Single – *You're the One That I Want* [Juno Award Canada]
Top Single – Duo – *You're the One That I Want* [*Record World* USA]
Most Outstanding Musical Achievement [*Musiek Parade Magazine* Holland]
Top Actress [Golden Hammer Awards Germany]

1979

Favourite Female Vocalist [People's Choice Awards USA]
Favourite Motion Picture Actress [People's Choice Awards USA]
Clio Award
Officer of the Order of the British Empire (OBE)

1980

Top Female Vocalist – Pop [National Jukebox Awards USA]

Top Actress [Golden Hammer Awards Germany]

1981
Star on Hollywood Boulevard 'Walk of Fame'

1982
Best Video – Long Form – *Physical* [Grammys USA]
Favourite Female Vocalist – Rock/Pop [American Music Awards]
No. 1 Artist of the Year – Singles [*Billboard Magazine*]
Favourite Female Vocalist – Pop [*Billboard Magazine*]
No. 1 Female Vocalist – Singles [*Cashbox Magazine* USA]

1989
Celebrity Businesswoman of the Year – Koala Blue [American Society of Retail Merchandisers]

1998
Cadillac concept Humanitarian Award [in recognition of her work towards breast cancer awareness]

1999
Red Cross Award

ALBUM SALES AWARDS

Gold Disc Awards

1973   *Let Me Be There* [MCA Records USA]
1974   *If You Love Me (Let Me Know)* [MCA Records USA]
1975   *Have You Never Been Mellow* [MCA Records USA]
1975   *Have You Never Been Mellow* [Festival Records Australia]
1975   *Clearly Love* [MCA Records USA]

1975 *Clearly Love* [Festival Records Australia]
1976 *Come on Over* [MCA Records USA]
1976 *Don't Stop Believin'* [MCA Records USA]
1976 *Don't Stop Believin'* [Festival Records Australia]
1980 Original Motion Picture Soundtrack *Xanadu* [JET Records UK]
1981 *Physical* [EMI Records UK]
1982 *Olivia's Greatest Hits* [EMI Records UK]
1985 *Soul Kiss* [MCA Records USA]
1985 *Soul Kiss* [Festival Records Australia]
1988 *The Rumour* [Festival Records Australia]
1992 *Back to Basics: The Essential Collection* [Geffen Records USA]
1994 *Gaia: One Woman's Journey* [Festival Records Australia]

Platinum Disc Awards

1971 *If Not For You* [Festival Records Australia]
1974 *First Impressions – Great Hits* [Festival Records Australia]
1974 *Long Live Love* [Festival Records Australia]
1977 *Greatest Hits Volume One* [MCA Records USA]
1977 *Greatest Hits Volume Two* [Festival Records Australia]
1978 Original Motion Picture Soundtrack *Grease* [RSO Records Worldwide]
1978 *Totally Hot* [MCA Records USA]
1978 *Totally Hot* [Festival Records Australia]
1980 Original Motion Picture Soundtrack *Xanadu* [MCA Records USA]
1980 Original Motion Picture Soundtrack *Xanadu* [Festival Records Australia]
1981 *Physical* [MCA Records USA]
1981 *Physical* [Festival Records Australia]
1982 *Olivia's Greatest Hits Volume Two* [MCA Records

USA]
1982 *Olivia's Greatest Hits Volume Three* [Festival Records Australia]
1983 Original Motion Picture Soundtrack *Two of a Kind* [MCA Records USA]
1992 *Back to Basics: The Essential Collection 1971–1992* [Festival Records Australia]
1998 *Highlights from 'The Main Event'* [BMG/RCA Australia]

CHART FILE

Singles

Year	Title	UK	USA	Australia
1971	'If Not For You'	7	25	14
1971	'Banks of the Ohio'	6	94	1 [3wks]
1972	'What is Life'	16	–	–
1973	'Take Me Home Country Roads'	15	119	–
1973	'Let Me Be There'	–	6	16
1974	'Long Live Love'	11	–	15
1974	'If You Love Me (Let Me Know)'	–	5	2
1974	'I Honestly Love You'	22	1 [4wks]	2
1975	'Have You Never Been Mellow'	–	1 [2wks]	12
1975	'Please Mr Please'	–	3	28
1975	'Something Better to Do'	–	13	71
1975	'Let it Shine'	–	30	54
1976	'Come on Over'	–	23	62

Year	Title	UK	USA	Australia
1976	'Don't Stop Believin''	–	33	–
1977	'Every Face Tells a Story'	–	55	–
1977	'Sam'	6	20	74
1977	'Making a Good Thing Better'	–	87	77
1978	'You're the One That I Want'	1 [9wks]	1 [1wk]	1 [6wks]
1978	'Jolene'	–	–	10
1978	'Summer Nights'	1 [7wks]	5	8
1978	'Hopelessly Devoted to You'	2	3	4
1978	'A Little More Love'	4	3	4
1979	'Deeper Than the Night'	64	11	71
1979	'Totally Hot'	–	52	96
1980	'Don't Cry for Me Argentina'	–	–	37
1980	'Xanadu'	1 [2wks]	8	2
1980	'Magic'	32	1 [4wks]	2
1980	'Suddenly'	15	20	26
1980	'I Can't Help It'	–	12	–
1981	'Physical'	7	1 [10wks]	1 [6wks]
1982	'Make a Move on Me'	43	5	17
1982	'Landslide'	18	52	42
1982	'Heart Attack'	46	3	–
1983	'I Honestly Love You'	52	–	–
1983	'Tied Up'	–	38	–
1983	'Twist of Fate'	57	5	17
1984	'Livin' in Desperate Times'	–	31	–
1985	'Soul Kiss'	–	20	12

Year	Title	UK	USA	Australia
1986	'Toughen Up'	–	–	69
1986	'The Best of Me'	–	80	–
1988	'The Rumour'	–	62	25
1990	'The Grease Megamix'	3	–	1 [4wks]
1991	'The Grease Dream Mix'	47	–	–
1992	'I Need Love'	75	96	–
1994	'No Matter What You Do'	–	–	30
1995	'Had To Be'	22	–	–
1998	'You're the One That I Want'	4	–	–
1998	'I Honestly Love You'	–	57	–

Albums

Year	Title	UK	USA	Australia
1971	*If Not For You*	–	158	14
1973	*Let Me Be There*	–	54	–
1974	*Music Makes My Day*	37	–	–
1974	*Long Live Love*	40	–	32
1974	*First Impressions – Great Hit*	–	–	1 [10wks]
1974	*If You Love Me (Let Me Know)*	–	1 [2wks]	–
1975	*Have You Never Been Mellow*	37	1 [1wk]	17
1975	*Clearly Love*	–	12	26
1976	*Come on Over*	–	13	30
1976	*Don't Stop Believin'*	–	30	44

Year	Title	UK	USA	Australia
1977	*Making a Good Thing Better*			
		60	34	–
1977	*Greatest Hits*	19	13	18
1978	*Grease* (OST)	1 [12wks]	1 [16wks]	1 [25wks]
1978	*Totally Hot*	30	7	4
1980	*Xanadu* (OST)	2	4	2
1981	*Physical*	11	6	1 [7wks]
1982	*Greatest Hits*	8	16	15
1983	*Two of a Kind* (OST)	–	26	35
1985	*Soul Kiss*	66	29	11
1988	*The Rumour*	–	67	15
1989	*Warm And Tender*	–	121	–
1990	*Grease* (OST)	9	–	1 [7wks]
1992	*Back to Basics: The Essential Collection*			
		12	126	2
1994	*Gaia: One Woman's Journey*			
		33	–	6
1995	*Songs from Heathcliff*	15	–	–
1998	*Back with a Heart*	–	59	56
1998	*Highlights from 'The Main Event'*			
		–	–	1[2wks]

ALBUM LISTINGS (TRACK BY TRACK)

Toomorrow
[RCA Records LSA 3008 – 1970]
'You're My Baby Now'; 'Taking Our Own Sweet Time'; 'Let's Move On'; 'If You Can't Be Hurt (You Can't Be Happy)'; 'Toomorrow'; 'Walking on Air'; 'Happiness Valley'; 'Going Back'.

Olivia Newton-John
[PYE International NSPL 28155 – 1971]
'Me and Bobby McGee'; 'If'; 'Banks of the Ohio'; 'In a Station'; 'Love Song'; 'Help Me Make it Through the Night'; 'If Not For You'; 'Where Are You Going to My Love'; 'Lullaby'; 'If You Could Read My Mind'; 'If I Gotta Leave'; 'No Regrets'.

Olivia
[PYE International NSPL 28168 – 1972]
'Angel of the Morning'; 'Just a Little Too Much'; 'If We Only Have Love'; 'Winterwood'; 'My Old Man's Got a Gun'; 'Changes'; 'I'm a Small and Lonely Light'; 'Why Don't You Write Me'; 'Mary Skeffington'; 'Behind That Locked Door'; 'What is Life'; 'Everything I Own'; 'Living in Harmony'; 'I Will Touch You'.

Let Me Be There
[MCA Records MCA 389 – 1973]
'Let Me Be There'; 'Me and Bobby McGee'; 'Banks of the Ohio'; 'Love Song'; 'If Not For You'; 'Take Me Home Country Roads'; 'Angel of the Morning'; 'If You Could Read My Mind'; 'Help Me Make it Through the Night'; 'Just a Little Too Much'.

Music Makes My Day
[PYE International NSPL 28185 – 1974]
'Take Me Home Country Roads'; 'Amoureuse'; 'Brotherly Love'; 'Heartbreaker'; 'Rosewater'; 'You Ain't Got the Right'; 'Feeling Best'; 'Being on the Losing End'; 'Let Me Be There'; 'Music Makes My Day'; 'Leaving'; 'If We Try'.

Long Live Love
[EMI Records EMC 3028 – 1974]
'Free the People'; 'Angel Eyes'; 'Country Girl'; 'Someday';

'God Only Knows'; 'Loving You Ain't Easy'; 'Home Ain't Home Anymore'; 'Have Love Will Travel'; 'I Honestly Love You'; 'Hands Across the Sea'; 'The River's Too Wide'; 'Long Live Love'.

First Impressions
[EMI Records EMC 3055 – 1974]
'If Not For You'; 'Banks of the Ohio'; 'Winterwood'; 'Take Me Home Country Roads'; 'Amoureuse'; 'Let Me Be There'; 'I Honestly Love You'; 'Long Live Love'; 'If You Love Me (Let Me Know)'; 'What is Life'; 'If We Try'; 'Music Makes My Day'.

If You Love Me (Let Me Know)
[MCA Records MCA 411 – 1974]
'If You Love Me (Let Me Know)'; 'Country Girl'; 'I Honestly Love You'; 'Mary Skeffington'; 'Free the People'; 'The River's Too Wide'; 'Home Ain't Home Anymore'; 'God Only Knows'; 'You Ain't Got the Right'; 'Changes'.

Have You Never Been Mellow
[EMI Records EMC 3069 – 1975]
'Have You Never Been Mellow'; 'Loving Arms'; 'Lifestream'; 'Goodbye Again'; 'Water Under the Bridge'; 'I Never Did Sing You a Love Song'; 'It's So Easy'; 'The Air That I Breathe'; 'Follow Me'; 'And in the Morning'; 'Please Mr Please'.

Clearly Love
[EMI Records EMA 774 – 1975]
'Something Better to Do'; 'Lovers'; 'Slow Down Jackson'; 'Summertime Blues'; 'Sail into Tomorrow'; 'Crying, Laughing, Loving, Lying'; 'Clearly Love'; 'He's My Rock'; 'Just a Lot of Folk (The Marshmallow Song)'; 'He Ain't Heavy… He's My Brother'; 'Let it Shine'.

Come on Over
[EMI Records EMC 3124 – 1976]
'Jolene'; 'Pony Ride'; 'Come on Over'; 'It'll Be Me';
'Greensleeves'; 'Blue Eyes Crying in the Rain'; 'Don't
Throw it All Away'; 'Who Are You Now?'; 'Smile for Me';
'Small Talk and Pride'; 'Wrap Me in Your Arms'; 'The
Long and Winding Road'.

Don't Stop Believin'
[EMI Records EMC 3162 – 1976]
'Don't Stop Believin'; 'A Thousand Conversations';
'Compassionate Man'; 'New Born Babe'; 'Hey Mr
Dreammaker'; 'Every Face Tells a Story'; 'Sam'; 'Love You
Hold the Key'; 'I'll Bet You a Kangaroo'; 'The Last Time
You Loved'.

Making a Good Thing Better
[EMI Records EMC 3192 – 1977]
'Making a Good Thing Better'; 'Slow Dancing'; 'Ring of
Fire'; 'Cooling Down'; 'Don't Cry for Me Argentina'; 'Sad
Songs'; 'You Won't See Me Cry'; 'So Easy to Begin'; 'I
Think I'll Say Goodbye'; 'Don't Ask a Friend'; 'If Love is
Real'.

Greatest Hits
[EMI Records EMA 785 – 1977]
'If Not For You'; 'Changes'; 'Let Me Be There'; 'If You
Love Me (Let Me Know)'; 'I Honestly Love You'; 'Have
You Never Been Mellow'; 'Please Mr Please'; 'Take Me
Home Country Roads'; 'Let it Shine'; 'Sam'; 'Don't Stop
Believin''.

Original Motion Picture Soundtrack *Grease* [Various]
[RSO Records RSD 2001 – 1978]
'Summer Nights' (with John Travolta and cast); 'Hope-

lessly Devoted to You'; 'You're the One That I Want' (with John Travolta); 'Look At Me, I'm Sandra Dee'; 'We Go Together' (with John Travolta and cast).

Totally Hot
[EMI Records EMA 789 – 1978]
'Please Don't Keep Me Waiting'; 'Dancin' Round and Round'; 'Talk To Me'; 'Deeper Than the Night'; 'Borrowed Time'; 'A Little More Love'; 'Never Enough'; 'Totally Hot'; 'Boats Against the Current'; 'Gimme Some Lovin''.

Original Motion Picture Soundtrack *Xanadu*
[JET Records LX 526 – 1980]
'Xanadu' (with ELO); 'Magic'; 'Suddenly' (with Cliff Richard); 'Dancin'' (with The Tubes); 'Suspended in Time'; 'Whenever You're Away from Me' (with Gene Kelly).

Physical
[EMI Records EMC 3386 – 1981]
'Landslide'; 'Stranger's Touch'; 'Make a Move on Me'; 'Falling'; 'Love Make Me Strong'; 'Physical'; 'Silvery Rain'; 'Carried Away'; 'Recovery'; 'The Promise (The Dolphin Song)'.

Olivia's Greatest Hits
[EMI Records EMTV 36 – 1982]
'Physical'; 'Deeper Than the Night'; 'A Little More Love'; 'Magic'; 'Heart Attack'; 'Make a Move on Me'; 'Tied Up'; 'Suddenly'; 'Changes'; 'If Not For You'; 'Banks of the Ohio'; 'Take Me Home Country Roads'; 'Sam'; 'I Honestly Love You'; 'Xanadu'; 'You're the One That I Want'; 'Summer Nights'; 'Hopelessly Devoted to You'; 'Landslide'; 'Rosewater'.

Original Motion Picture Soundtrack *Two of a Kind*
[Various]
[EMI Records EMC 1654614 – 1983]
'Twist of Fate'; 'Take a Chance' (with John Travolta);
'Shaking You'; '(Livin' in) Desperate Times'.

Soul Kiss
[Mercury Records MERH 77 – 1985]
'Toughen Up'; 'Soul Kiss'; 'Queen of the Publication';
'Emotional Tangle'; 'Culture Shock'; 'Moth to a Flame';
'Overnight Observation'; 'You Were Great, How Was I?'
(with Carl Wilson); 'Driving Music'; 'Electric'; 'The Right
Moment'.

The Rumour
[Mercury Records MER 834 9571 – 1988]
'The Rumour'; 'Can't We Talk it Over in Bed'; 'Love and
Let Live'; 'Let's Talk About Tomorrow'; 'It's Not Heaven';
'Get Out'; 'Big and Strong'; 'Car Games'; 'Walk Through
Fire'; 'Tutta La Vita'.

Love Songs
[MFP CD 6042 – 1988]
'Please Mr Please'; 'Have You Never Been Mellow'; 'If';
'Angel of the Morning'; 'Behind That Locked Door'; 'God
Only Knows'; 'Love Song'; 'No Regrets'; 'If You Could
Read My Mind'; 'I Honestly Love You'; 'Amoureuse';
'Where Are You Going to My Love'; 'Lullaby'; 'I Will
Touch You'; 'Winterwood'; 'If We Only Have Love';
'Changes'.

Warm And Tender
[Mercury Records MER 842 1452 – 1989]
'Jenny Rebecca'; 'Rocking'; 'The Way You Look Tonight';
'Lullaby My Lovely'; 'You'll Never Walk Alone'; 'Sleep My

Princess'; 'The Flower That Shattered the Stone'; 'Twinkle, Twinkle Little Star'; 'Warm and Tender'; 'Rock-a-bye Baby'; 'Over the Rainbow'; 'The Twelfth of Never'; 'All the Pretty Little Horses'; 'When You Wish Upon a Star'; 'Reach Out for Me'; 'Brahm's Lullaby'.

Back to Basics: The Essential Collection 1971–1992
[Mercury Records MER 5126412 – 1992]
'If Not For You'; 'Banks of the Ohio'; 'What is Life'; 'Take Me Home Country Roads'; 'I Honestly Love You'; 'Have You Never Been Mellow'; 'Sam'; 'You're the One That I Want'; 'Summer Nights'; 'Hopelessly Devoted to You'; 'A Little More Love'; 'Xanadu'; 'Magic'; 'Suddenly'; 'Physical'; 'The Rumour';, I Need Love'; 'Deeper Than a River'; 'I Want to Be Wanted'; 'Not Gonna Be the One'.

48 Original Tracks
[EMI Records CDEM 1503 – 1994]
'Love Song'; 'Banks of the Ohio'; 'Me and Bobby McGee'; 'If Not For You'; 'Help Me Make it Through the Night'; 'If You Could Read My Mind'; 'In a Station'; 'Where Are You Going to My Love'; 'Lullaby'; 'No Regrets'; 'If I Gotta Leave'; 'Would You Follow Me'; 'Changes'; 'Everything I Own'; 'If'; 'It's So Hard to Say Goodbye'; 'Winterwood'; 'What is Life'; 'I'm a Small and Lonely Light'; 'Just a Little Too Much'; 'Living in Harmony'; 'Why Don't You Write Me'; 'Angel of the Morning'; 'Mary Skeffington'; 'If We Only Have Love'; 'My Old Man's Got a Gun'; 'Maybe Then I'll Think of You'; 'Amoureuse'; 'Take Me Home Country Roads'; 'I Honestly Love You'; 'Music Makes My Day'; 'Heartbreaker'; 'Leaving'; 'You Ain't Got the Right'; 'Feeling Best'; 'Rosewater'; 'Being on the Losing End'; 'If We Try'; 'Let Me Be There'; 'Country Girl'; 'Loving You Ain't Easy'; 'Have Love Will Travel'; 'Hands Across the Sea'; 'Please Mr Please'; 'The Air That I Breathe'; 'Loving

Arms'; 'If You Love Me (Let Me Know)'; 'Have You Never Been Mellow'.

Gaia: One Woman's Journey
[D# DHS LCD 7017 – 1995]
'Trust Yourself'; 'No Matter What You Do'; 'No Other Love'; 'Pegasus'; 'Why Me?'; 'Don't Cut Me Down'; 'Gaia'; 'Do You Feel?'; 'I Never Knew Love'; 'Silent Ruin'; 'Not Gonna Give into It'; 'The Way of Love'.

Songs from Heathcliff (With Cliff Richard)
[EMI Records CDEMD 1091 – 1995]
'Had To Be'; 'Dream Tomorrow'; 'I Do Not Love You Isabella'; 'Choosing When it's Too Late'; 'Marked with Death'.

The Singles (Australasian Tour Souvenir)
[Festival Records TVD 93488 – 1998]
As 'Back to Basics' collection – plus bonus compact disc:–
'No Matter What You Do'; 'Don't Cut Me Down'; 'It's Always Australia for Me'; 'Can't We Talk it Over in Bed'; 'The Rumour'; 'Please Mr Please'; 'Jolene'; 'Don't Cry for Me Argentina'; 'Heart Attack'; 'Toughen Up'.

Back with a Heart
[MCA/Universal Records UMD 80487 – 1998]
'Precious Love'; 'Closer To Me'; 'Fight for Our Love'; 'Spinning His Wheels'; 'Under My Skin'; 'Love is a Gift'; 'I Don't Wanna Say Good Night'; 'Don't Say That'; 'Attention'; 'Back with a Heart'; 'I Honestly Love You'.

Country Girl
[EMI Records 495 9702 – 1998]
'Love Song'; 'Banks of the Ohio'; 'If Not For You'; 'If You Could Read My Mind'; 'Lullaby'; 'It's So Hard to Say

Goodbye'; 'Winterwood'; 'What is Life'; 'Changes'; 'Living in Harmony'; 'If We Only Have Love'; 'Take Me Home Country Roads'; 'I Honestly Love You'; 'Music Makes My Day'; 'Rosewater'; 'Let Me Be There'; 'Please Mr Please'; 'The Air That I Breathe'; 'If You Love Me (Let Me Know)'; 'Have You Never Been Mellow'.

The Very Best of...
[EMI Records 4945632 – 1998]
'Banks of the Ohio'; 'If Not For You'; 'I Honestly Love You'; 'What is Life'; 'Take Me Home Country Roads'; 'Long Live Love'; 'Love Song'; 'The Air That I Breathe'; 'Me and Bobby McGee'; 'Help Me Make it Through the Night'; 'If You Love Me (Let Me Know)'; 'Have You Never Been Mellow'; 'Please Mr Please'; 'If'; 'Angel of the Morning'; 'Let Me Be There'; 'A Little More Love'; 'Everything I Own'.

Highlights from 'The Main Event' – Australian Tour with John Farnham and Antony Warlow
[BMG/RCA Records 74321638832 – 1998]
'Overture'; 'Age of Reason'; 'Phantom of the Opera'; 'A Little More Love'; 'Age of Reason'; 'This is the Moment'; 'Hopelessly Devoted to You'; 'Every Time You Cry'; 'Please Don't Ask Me'; 'You're the One That I Want'; 'The Long and Winding Road'; 'Take Me Home Country Roads'; 'I Honestly Love You'; 'Love is a Gift'; 'That's Life/Bad Habits'; 'Granada'; 'You've Lost That Loving Feeling'; 'Summer Nights'; 'If Not for You'; 'Let Me Be There'; 'Raindrops Keep Falling on My Head'; 'Jolene'; 'Hearts on Fire'; 'Don't You Know it's Magic'; 'You're the Voice'.

Funny Things Happen Down Under
1965 Pacific Films. Dir: Joe McCormick. Prod: Roger Mirams. Cast: Sue Howarth, Ian Turpie, Bruce Barrie, Howard Morrison, Olivia Newton-John, Gary Gray and the Terrible Ten.

Toomorrow
1970 Rank Organization. Dir: Val Guest. Prod: Harry Saltzman and Don Kirschner. Cast: Benny Thomas, Olivia Newton-John, Vic Cooper, Karl Chambers and Roy Dotrice.

Grease
1978 Paramount Pictures. Dir: Randal Kleiser. Prod: Alan Carr and Robert Stigwood. Cast: John Travolta, Olivia Newton-John, Stockard Channing, Jeff Conway, Didi Conn and Eve Arden. [CIC video VHR 2003 and VHR 2626 wide screen]

Xanadu
1980 Universal Pictures. Dir: Robert Greenwald. Prod: Larry Gordon. Cast: Olivia Newton-John, Gene Kelly and Michael Beck. [CIC video VHR 1018]

Two of a Kind
1983 Twentieth Century Fox Pictures. Dir: John Hertzfeld. Prod: Joe Wizan and Roger M. Rothstein. Cast: John Travolta, Olivia Newton-John, Oliver Reed, Beatrice Straight, Scatman Crothers and Charles Durning. [CBS/FOX video VHS 1339-50]

A Mom for Christmas
1990 Buena Vista Productions. Dir: George Miller. Prod:

Steve White and Barry Bernardi. Cast: Olivia Newton-John, Juliet Scorcey, Doug Sheehan, Doris Roberts and Carmen Argeziano. [Walt Disney Home Video D140822]

A Christmas Romance
1994 Spectator Films. Director and producer: Sheldon Larry. Cast: Olivia Newton-John, Gregory Harrison and Chloe Lattanzi. [Odyssey video ODY 446]

It's My Party
1995 United Artists Pictures. Dir: Randal Kleiser. Prod: Robert Fitzpatrick, Gregory Hinton and Joel Thurm. Cast: Margaret Cho, Bruce Davison, Lee Grant, Gregory Harrison, Marlee Matlin, Roddy McDowell, Olivia Newton-John, Bronson Pinchot and Eric Roberts. [MGM/UA video VO55527]

MUSIC VIDEOS

Physical [EMI Music Videos TVE 90 05312 – 1981]
Live! [Embassy Home Video/Channel 5 CFV 00522 – 1982]
Twist of Fate – EP [EMI MVS 99 00072 – 1983]
Soul Kiss – Videosingles [Polygram Video 041 4252 – 1985]
Down Under [Polygram Music Video CFV 02572 – 1988]

MISCELLANEOUS VIDEOS

Olivia Newton-John's 'Animal Friends' [Australian Festival Videos V82758 – 1999]
Olivia Newton-John's 'Australia's Amazing Animals' [Australian Festival Videos V82759 –1999]
Olivia Newton-John's 'Exotic Animals' [Australian Festival

Videos V82760 – 1999]

Olivia Newton-John's 'Under the Surf' [Australian Festival Videos V82761 – 1999]

And I Quote…

John Travolta (actor)
'She is a force to be dealt with, definitely her own woman. She knows what she wants and she goes after it. At the same time managing to stay totally feminine and sexy!'

Alan Thicke (TV producer)
'She can be very tough, but she does it with such grace and respect for your point of view that you walk away and don't realise for two days that she won her point.'

Larry Gordon (producer *Xanadu*)
'We all know she's as smart as hell and a great star! I'd like to do all of her pictures, and I can't give her higher praise than that. She has temperament; but she's so damned nice – everyone wants to work for her.'

Gene Kelly (actor)
'She's charming, lovely and a delight to work with.'

Sir Cliff Richard (singer)
'Olivia has more sex appeal in her little finger than Madonna has in her whole body!'

George Miller (film producer)
'Olivia Newton-John – I describe as "one of the great smiles of the twentieth century".'

John Farrar (record producer)
'The number one thing that she's got going for her is her ability to communicate lyrics to people. I think a lot of people believe that she's singing the songs to them – personally.'

Matt Lattanzi (ex-husband)
'I don't think our child could have a better mother. She was born to be a mother. She's always talked about having children – it was just timing.'

Olivia Newton-John
'I suppose my dreams were to have a hit record. I mean, that would be when I first started recording. That seemed to be the highest goal I could reach.'

Nicky Campbell (BBC radio presenter)
'If I'd known back in 1981 [when I was fifteen years old] that I would one day be interviewing Olivia Newton-John – I would have gone blind instantly! She just oozed pure aerobic sex!'

Nancy Gould Chuda (friend and co-founder of CHEC)
'The first day Livvy came home from chemotherapy – she looked so drawn and thin – and my heart just broke! It was just remembering everything my daughter, Colette, went through – and for me, it was so traumatic to have to watch my best friend go through it as well!'

Cole Joy (Australian rock veteran)
'Olivia's direction was right. She did what she's always done best – she sings well and she has been a good world citizen.'

Dionne Warwick (singer)

'The description I have always had for Olivia's voice is 'crystal' – because it is so crystal clear. She has a beautiful voice and she uses it well!'

Bibliography

Altman, Linda Jacobs, *Olivia Newton-John – Sunshine Supergirl*, n.p., 1975

Branson-Trent, Gregory *More Than Physical!*, Canada, Collector's Guide Publishing, 1994

Clarkson, Wensley, *John Travolta: Back in Character*, n.p., 1996

Coleman, Ray, *The Carpenters Story*, UK, Boxtree Ltd, 1995

Conn, Didi, *Frenchy's* Grease *Scrapbook*, USA, Chameleon Books, 1998

Emery, Ralph, *The View from Nashville*, USA, Morrow Books, 1998

Kelly, Gene, *My Life*, n.p., 1988

Morse, Anne *Olivia Newton-John*, n.p., 1976

Newton-John, Olivia, and Seth Hurst, Brian, *A Pig Tale*, USA, Simon & Schuster, 1993

Ruff, Peter *Olivia Newton-John*, USA, Quickfox, 1979

Turner, Tina *I, Tina*, n.p., 1987

Welch, Bruce, *Rock 'n' Roll – I Gave You the Best Years of My Life*, UK, Viking Books, 1989

Zanderbergen, George, *Singing Sweetly: Cher, Olivia Newton-John and Roberta Flack*, n.p., 1976

Further Information

ADDRESSES OF THE 'ONLY OLIVIA' FAN CLUB

PO Box 388, Ipswich IP4 4HR, UK
PO Box 131044, Ann Arbor, MI 48113 - 1044, USA
PO Box 483, Curtin, Canberra, ACT 2605, Australia

World Wide Web site: http://www.onlyolivia.com/

A portion of proceeds from the sale of this book will be donated to the Children's Health Environmental Coalition (CHEC): CHEC, Po Box 846, Malibu CALIF 90265.